Letters from Baghdad

An Iraq War Diary

By

Lt. Col. David G. Conklin (Ret.)

Copyright © 2023 by David G. Conklin

All rights reserved.

Permission to reproduce in any form
must be secured from the author.

Please direct all correspondence and book orders to:

David G. Conklin
965 Ranch Lane
Kalispell, MT 59901
Tel: 406-210-4989
conklind@hotmail.com

Library of Congress Control Number: 2023952591

ISBN 978-1-7362441-4-2

Printed for the author by
Moore Graphics
11200 W. Wisconsin Ave. #6
Youngtown, AZ 85363

Cover photos:
Front: *Desert Sandstorm near Presidential Palace, Baghdad, 2004*
Back: *Crossed Sabers Park, Baghdad, 2004*

This book is dedicated to the brave and selfless men and women of the 350th Civil Affairs Command, as well as the countless reservists, National Guard members, and civilians who volunteer for duty to support our troops whenever and wherever they are deployed.

And:

To my father and grandfather, Charles F. Conklin, and Charles W. Conklin who served our country building Liberty ships in World War II;

to my great-grandfather Josiah Conklin, a soldier in the Civil War;

to my great-great-grandfather Abraham John Conklin, a soldier in the War of 1812;

and to his father Abraham Conklin, a soldier in the Revolutionary War.

SSG Dave Conklin, 350th Civil Affairs Command, 2004

Dave Conklin, defense contractor, 2005

CONTENTS

Introduction 1

Part 1. 2004 - My War as an Army Reservist 9

  1. On Your Mark, Get Ready, Mobilize! 9

  2. On to Kuwait 22

  3. Welcome to Baghdad 29

  4. Baghdad Winter 45

  5. The Coming Storm 63

  6. The Desert Heats Up 84

  7. Approaching the Speed of Sovereignty 94

  8. A New Government is Born 107

  9. Summer in the City 116

  10. Getting Short 138

  11. Return to Kuwait 152

Part 2. 2005 - My War as a Defense Contractor 163

  12. Return to Iraq 163

  13. Back to the Front 171

  14. Spring Travels 175

  15. Summer Attacks 181

  16. Prelude to Ramadan 192

  17. The Fight Goes On 200

    Acknowledgements 207

Glossary	208
References	210
Index	211
About the Author	215

Introduction

This book offers a unique perspective of the Iraq War through my daily journal, in which I describe firsthand my personal perspective of the horrors of war while deployed to Baghdad as an American soldier during the year 2004 and later in 2005 after I became a civilian contractor. It also provides a glimpse of my experiences and thoughts as I muse, sometimes seriously, sometimes sarcastically, about the individual human experience of daily life in a war zone. This journal also includes my eyewitness photos of these times and events as I described them to my family and friends back home.

My purpose in writing this book is primarily to provide some closure to the events I witnessed or participated in during the Iraq War. Some veterans go their entire lives without ever discussing their experiences, as did my Uncle Ervin Schmale, a sailor in World War II. I can't imagine the memories he may have kept bottled up inside. As for me, I mentally dealt with these events by keeping a daily journal when I could. I felt the urge to write something before I could let go of the events of the day and before I turned in for the night. Not that I necessarily WANTED TO write about the event, I HAD TO write about it, or it would fester in my subconscious until I got it out by writing about it.

Sometimes I would write about my daily routine or offer comments about the food, the rules, or poke fun at my colleagues. In other entries I describe in detail mortar attacks, ambushes, and being shot at. One mortar attack I described in Chapter 10 (September 13, 2004) involved SGT Tina Beller, one of my colleagues at the 350th Civil Affairs Command. Her letter to her parents about this attack was later published in *Operation Homecoming* (Carroll, 2006, pp. 261-265). For security reasons I would often write and date a journal entry but wait several days before sending it to my family.

But why I ended up being a part of the Iraq War goes back many years. In 1969, during the height of the unpopular Vietnam War, I joined the ROTC (Reserve Officer Training Corps) program at my college to deploy and find out why the war was so unpopular. I completed basic training at Fort Benning, Georgia where I found that the overwhelming majority of recruits, unlike me, were draftees who did not have the funds to go to college and get a deferment. I will never forget that our army was manned and led by the poorest of our citizens. I did not disagree with the draft, but I did disagree with the deferments.

But by the time my own college deferment was up and I graduated, the war was ending, deployments had stopped, the draft had ended, and I became a reserve officer for the next 28 years. Career and family occupied those years. I retired as a Lieutenant Colonel in 1999 but re-enlisted as a Sergeant to become a Broadcast Journalist. As a sergeant I was reminded that enlisted troops are at the mercy of their leaders, and so I promised myself if there was another war before I retired, I would volunteer to help our soldiers stay alive however I could. I got my chance during another unpopular war: Operation Iraqi Freedom. In 2004 I was near retirement at age 56, my wife was working, and my children were grown, so I felt that I could face the very real possibility of being killed or wounded better than the younger soldiers. So when a reservist colleague asked me to join him and deploy to Iraq, I transferred from the Army National Guard to the Army Reserve and deployed with them, even though I disagreed with our country being involved in the war.

Also, I must admit that as Winston Churchill once said, "There is nothing so exhilarating as being shot at and missed." (Carroll, 2006, p. xxii). That may have something to do with the nickname "Danger Dave" I received from my colleagues (see Chapter 17, November 13, 2005).

Book Format

This Introduction provides the context of the journals, including a brief look at the Iraq War and my life. The book is divided into two parts. Part I covers my military deployment as an Army Reserve Staff Sergeant in 2004. I use the original format, dividing the journal into chapters by timeframe, and within each chapter, dividing the original journal entries by location, time and time zone, day, and date written to make it easier for the reader to follow the action. Part II covers my civilian deployment as a defense contractor representative in 2005. Again I use the original format, dividing the journal into chapters and journal entries by subject, location, time and time zone, day, and date written.

My journal entries and digital photos were created during or shortly after the events they describe. The entries have not been "polished" or changed since they were sent as letters, e-mails, and attachments. The only reformatting done was to take the separate e-mail messages and develop a layout to combine them into a "journal." As such, it includes my firsthand opinions as well as the real names of the participants. The only other changes to the format include correcting misspellings or military rank abbreviations, and adding the proper names for acronyms (i.e. Operation Iraqi Freedom for OIF) where necessary. Brackets [ ] are used where I have added text necessary to correct the word flow or to explain or identify a phrase. Finally, a Glossary of Military Acronyms & Abbreviations, References and an Index are provided.

Map of Iraq –Courtesy of Nations Online Project.

Operation Iraqi Freedom

Operation Iraqi Freedom (OIF), commonly known as the Iraq War, was a full-scale invasion of Iraq by a U.S.-led coalition force of more than 260,000 troops. Arguably one of the best executed military campaigns in the last 70 years, the result was total domination by the Coalition forces. In less than 40 days the Coalition crushed the Iraqi Army, captured the capital of Baghdad, and removed the regime of Saddam Hussein.

This successful invasion and occupation of Iraq was part of the U.S. reaction to the terrorist attacks of September 11, 2001, after which the U.S. claimed Iraq had broken UN sanctions, sponsored terrorist groups, and possessed weapons of mass destruction. The Coalition faced an Iraqi Army estimated to have 400,000 troops, inflicting heavy casualties on them while Coalition U.S. casualties were fewer than 130 (Jorgensen, 2012, p. 251).

However lack of planning for the resulting occupation of Iraq ignored a spiraling insurgency that accounted for several thousand deaths every month in Baghdad alone. By mid-April 2004, during my deployment, it was already the deadliest month for U.S. troops in Iraq. The U.S. death toll had climbed to 134, more than the number of troops killed in the war's opening stages, from the invasion to the toppling of Saddam Hussein in Baghdad. *See: Iraq's Deadliest Month* (Zoroya, 2004, p. 1).

Also Coalition military actions alienated large setions of the Iraqi public. There is evidence that around 30,000 Iraqi civilians were killed by the indiscriminate use of firepower by U.S. troops in just the first 40 days of the war (Jorgensen, 2012, p. 251). After the invasion the disbandment of the Iraqi army created an explosion of intertribal and interfaith conflicts which took many lives of both Coalition personnel and Iraqi civilians alike. Operation Iraqi Freedom (OIF) officially began March 20, 2003 and ended December 15, 2011.

Author Biography

LTC David Conklin (Ret.), has authored numerous books and magazine articles, and most recently is the editor and translator of *Mexico's De la Huerta Rebellion: A Veteran's Chronicle* (Guerra, 2021).

Known as Dave, he was born in Lynwood and raised in South Gate, California. Upon graduation from high school in 1966, his family moved to Spokane, Washington where his father moved his Atlantic Mattress Company and started Northwest Bedding Company. Dave loved the outdoors and set his sights on becoming a forest ranger. He graduated from the University of Idaho in 1970 with a BS in Forestry, and the University of Montana in 1972 with an MS in Natural Resources and later an MBA.

He married Mary Guerra from Boise, Idaho in 1969 while in college. Their daughter Dacia was born the next year. In 1972 they moved to Helena, Montana to start his 27-year career in state parks while Mary worked for the Legislative Council. While working as a Park Ranger they moved to Miles City where their son Christopher was born in 1982. They returned to Helena in 1983 where Dave became Chief of Park Operations, and in 1990 they moved to Kalispell where he retired in 1999 at age 50 and began consulting and writing travel books until volunteering for military service in Iraq in 2004.

Even though his draft card lottery number was 348 he joined the Reserve Officer Training Command in 1969 during his senior year in college and was commissioned an officer in the U.S. Army Reserve, Corps of Engineers in 1971. He continued to serve for 37 years, retiring as a Lieutenant Colonel in 2008. Along the way he served as an exchange officer with the German Army and on a Military Liaison Team in Bulgaria. From 1997 to 1999 Conklin served as Deputy Chief of the Military Liaison Team (MLT) to Bulgaria for the Joint Contact Team Program (JCTP) of the United States European Command. As such he assisted in U.S. peacetime engagement activities with the Bulgarian armed forces.

Conklin's previous assignments include: Assistant Director of Military Support, Assistant Facilities Management Officer; Plans, Operations & Military Support Officer, Montana Army National Guard (ARNG); and Assistant Regimental, Regimental, and Brigade Engineer for the 163rd Armored Cavalry, ARNG. In 1989 Conklin served as a National Guard Exchange Officer to the Federal Republic of Germany. He is an honor graduate of both U.S. Army Command & General Staff College and the Defense Information School. His foreign languages include Bulgarian, Spanish, German, and Arabic.

After his service as a commissioned officer Conklin re-enlisted in 1999 becoming an Army Staff Sergeant and Non-Commissioned Officer in Charge (NCOIC) of the Montana Broadcast Section of the 111th Press Camp from 1999 to 2003 where he supervised developing, scheduling, and executing Audio/Visual Section productions. At age 56 he volunteered for mobilization to Iraq in 2004 as both Public Affairs and Finance Section NCOIC for the 350th Civil Affairs Command. When he retired in 2008 at the age of 60, SSG Conklin was the NCO for the 9th MSC PAO Section at Fort Shafter, Hawaii.

His Military Occupation Specialties (MOS) included 46Q, 46R, 42A, 42L, and 12B. His military decorations include the Bronze Star, Defense Meritorious Service Medal, four Army Commendation Medals, the Iraq Campaign Medal, and the Combat Action Badge as well as numerous others.

In his last civilian occupation before retiring, Conklin was a U.S. Department of Defense contractor in Iraq and S.W. Asia. After returning from Iraq in 2004 Dave was recruited by Tapestry Solutions, Inc., a logistics information technology company and spent the next 10 years as a military defense contractor training soldiers, Marines and security contractors in Iraq, Japan, Korea, Thailand, Philippines, Australia, and the U.S. Conklin moved with his wife Mary to Hawaii for 7 years and to Camp Pendleton, California for 2 years before retiring for a third time at age 65. Dave and Mary then bought a winter home in Arizona where he is active in hiking, travel, and writing.

Author Sketch Maps

The following two pages are sketch maps of portions of the city of Baghdad that I made during my deployment to Iraq which show the relationship of important locations in my area of operations which are mentioned in the narrative. On the first map I have outlined in bold the "Green Zone," Baghdad International Airport (BIAP), and the road (route Irish) that we used when driving from one to another.

The second sketch map shows a portion of central Baghdad on which I have outlined the Green Zone, the main roads we used to get around in it, the Joint Contracting Office where I worked, and the names and numbers of each entry control point, or checkpoint (CP), into the Green Zone which we and our Iraqi staff used to come in and out, and which we used to meet our customers and contractors. Sometimes I needed to know which gate to meet up with our contractors in order to receive the goods we requisitioned.

Letters from Baghdad 7

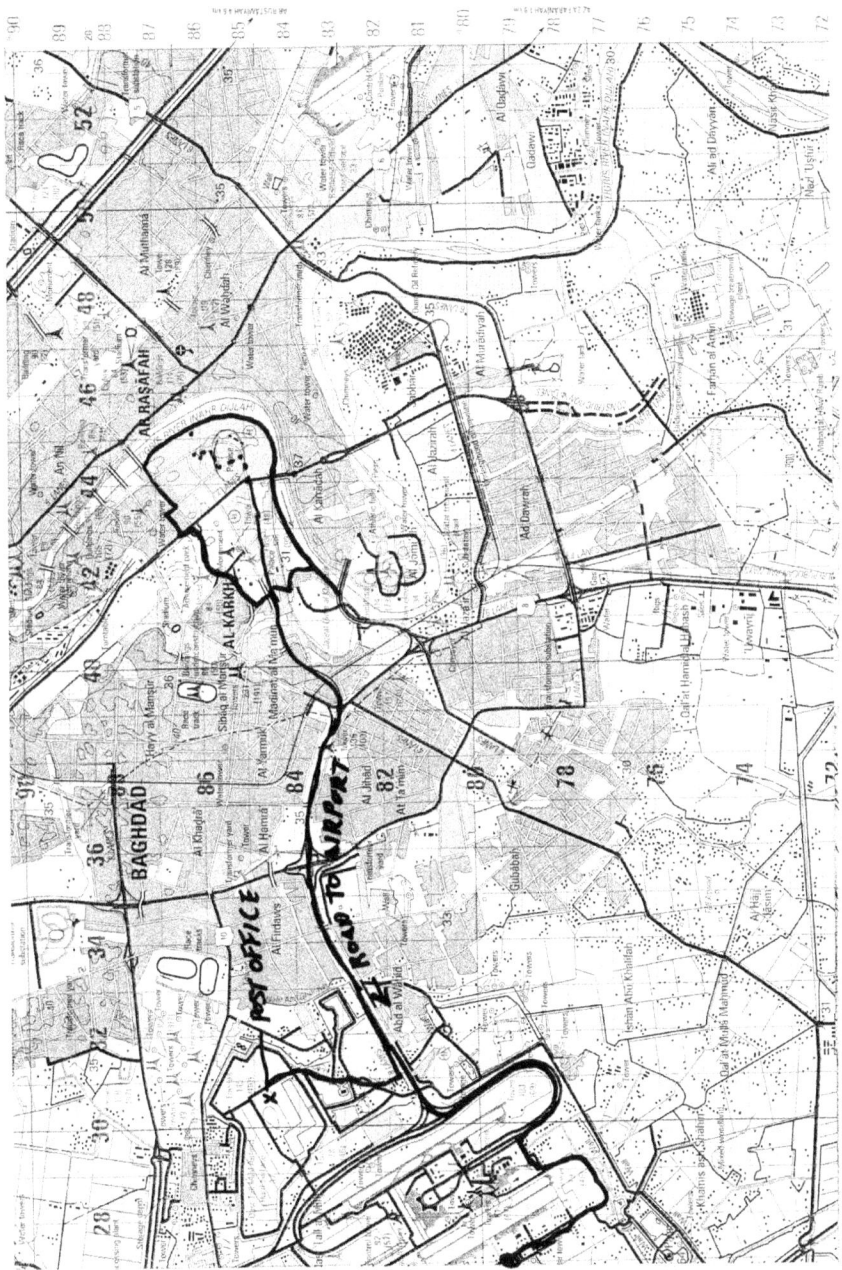

Map of central Baghdad showing the Green Zone highlighted on the right (top) and BIAP on the left and the airport road connecting them. April 11, 2004.

Map of central Baghdad showing the Green Zone along with names and numbers of each entry control point or checkpoint (CP). The Joint Contracting Office is marked with an asterisk on the right (top). April 11, 2004.

Part 1. 2004 - My War as an Army Reservist

1. On Your Mark, Get Ready, Mobilize!

Whitefish, Montana, 1400 Hours Tango, Monday, 12Jan2004
My cell phone rang as I skied off the Hellroaring chairlift on one of those rare crystal clear days at Big Mountain. It was the call I had been expecting from the 350th Civil Affairs Command in Pensacola, Florida. BJ said she had my mobilization orders for Operation Iraqi Freedom (OIF) and would fax my itinerary for my plane ticket to link up with the rest of my unit at Fort Bragg tomorrow. Colonel John Domenech, an old friend from my days in the Montana National Guard, had requested my transfer to the 350th as they were headed for Baghdad and needed some more experienced people who could help in the huge task of rebuilding Iraq. So here I was headed overseas again for God and country, guts and glory, and all that stuff. I guess tonight I'd better finish packing my duffle bag, make a CD with my files, and find an Arabic language book.

Whitefish, Montana, 0830 Hours Tango, Tuesday, 13Jan2004
Mary cried when I kissed her goodbye, and I felt guilty that I didn't. Even though we have both been through this before it is never easy to say goodbye when you don't know when, or even if, you will return. So I simply try to block out the "what ifs" and think of each deployment as an adventure, a kind of vacation with a bunch of guys with guns. The General says we will be deployed for about 9 months, but my orders say 365 days. Others in my unit have orders that read 550 days. The truth is, we won't really know until we get back home, and our time in Iraq will in all likelihood depend on how well the operation goes and when they can get another unit to replace us when we leave.

Old Division Area, Fort Bragg, North Carolina, 0900 Hours Romeo, Wednesday, 14Jan2004

Colonel Dan Magill, the Command G1 (personnel) met me at the Fayetteville airport late last night. Colonel Dan had been on active duty for nearly a year already. He was a federal ATF agent in his civilian job in Gainesville, Florida. But for the past year he's the guy who had the job of recruiting and filling battle roster vacancies with people recommended by guys like Colonel Domenech. I checked in at the temporary office, Building 4658 and caught a ride to my barracks, Building 5250, an old two-story World War II open bay barracks with bunk beds and beat-up lockers. But it did have heat and running water. In fact, the water couldn't be completely shut off in the toilets and sinks. Since I was already 10 days behind, I quickly changed into my BDUs and reported to the administration office to begin my "in-processing."

Specialist Jason Copeland holds the unit guidon during a noon formation outside the Old Division Area barracks at Fort Bragg, North Carolina Tuesday Jan 20, 2004. (DCP01909) (Photo --Dave Conklin)

Fort Bragg, North Carolina, 1400 Hours Romeo, Thursday, 15Jan2004

Fort Bragg is the home of the 18th Airborne Corps and the 82nd Airborne Division, most of whom are in Iraq right now. The fort is also the headquarters of the Special Operations Command (SOC) that includes Special Forces and our command, the Civil Affairs and Psychological Operations Command (CAPOC), of which 85% are reservists in specialized occupations such as lawyers, doctors, electrical engineers, and other specialists. With 70,000 troops and support personnel, Fort Bragg overshadows the nearby community of Fayetteville. Maybe that's why the locals on post refer to Fayetteville as "Fayette-nam."

Major Shawn Bell, behind guidon, poses with 350th Bosnia veterans at the Old Division Area barracks at Fort Bragg, North Carolina Wednesday Jan 21, 2004. (DCP01911) (Photo --Dave Conklin)

Today is push day for me and two other late arrivals, Major Bell and Staff Sergeant Joe Vovchik, who are transfers from the 486th Civil Affairs Battalion in Tulsa, Oklahoma. We skip the "required" initial day-long briefings for later and bum a ride to get ID cards, then straight to the clinic for a battery of tests, checkups, dental x-rays, and shots. Despite what I have always told my wife, they say my hearing is excellent. For shots, I get two in one arm and three in the other, including smallpox, anthrax, typhoid, flu, and tuberculosis. We arrived early and were out by noon.

Platoon sergeant Dees then arranged a ride for the three of us to CIF (central issue facility), where during a lull between units, we got a shopping cart full of desert camouflage uniforms (DCUs), t-shirts, drawers, socks, three sets of polypro underwear, a field jacket, patrol cap, "boonie" hat, helmet cover, two pairs of suede boots, one pair of cold weather Matterhorn boots, a 2-quart canteen, and interceptor body armor (IBA). Of course if they don't have your size, you can either grow, shrink, or go without. So I got a mix of "medium regular" DCUs (they said they would shrink), a small field jacket, 9R desert boots, and 9W winter boots. I figured if anything didn't fit, at least I might be able to trade when I got to where I was going. For those of us who didn't have a chance to draw our "TA-50" personal equipment back at the unit, the next stop was CIF. Here each of us signed for a Kevlar helmet, rucksack, rain jacket, canteen, load bearing equipment (LBE) vest and two duffle bags. Later we sent our uniforms with the supply sergeant to get our patches and nametapes sewn on at a shop outside the post.

Old Division Area, Fort Bragg, 0800 Hours Romeo, Friday, 16Jan2004

Back at the barracks supply Sergeant Ortiz began issuing us the rest of the equipment he brought from the unit. This included a plastic footlocker with assorted goodies inside like foot powder, a gun cleaning kit, seven M16 thirty-round magazines, towels, two pair of goggles, one pair of Wylie-X sunglasses, insect repellent, suntan lotion, plastic baggies, a signal mirror, and a folding stool. Then we got a duffle bag with a poncho, poncho liner, sleeping bag and cover, foam pad, canteen, gas mask, the new J-LIST (Joint Light Integrated Suit Technology) chemical suit, a camelback 3-liter water pack, and a "spear" suit which is a 4-layer cold weather suit and includes polyester underwear and a fleece jacket. The J-LIST consists of rubber boots and two packs of clothing that look like oversize vacuum-packed MREs.

Today we travel with the unit to draw weapons, mine being an M16 A2 rifle, while officers draw M9 9mm pistols. Most of the troops will be on the "reflexive fire" range today and the "convoy" live fire range tomorrow. Three of us will split off and join other units who are "zeroing" their rifles, and then we "qualify" on our new weapons on the record fire

Weapons clearing barrel outside the Old Division Area Barracks at Fort Bragg, North Carolina Friday Jan 16, 2004. DCP01914) (Photo --Dave Conklin)

range. I qualify with my first 40 rounds, but my battle buddy needs 240 rounds to finish the task. The bus driver tells us that the soldiers at Fort Bragg use the easier paper target range rather than this pop-up target range to qualify whenever they can. We return to the range in the evening for night firing on the record fire range. When we get back to our barracks, I borrow some cold medicine and vitamins from our chaplain and collapse into my cot as my cold has gotten worse each day I have been here.

Peck Field, Fort Bragg, 0730 Hours Romeo, Saturday, 17Jan2004

The dawn broke sunny and cold again, and the temperature stood at 25 F as the three of us reached the gas chamber at the edge of Peck Field. Inside the building, a combination of tear gas and sulfur would verify whether our gas masks were sealing properly. We put on our masks and then entered the building. We went through a series of drills including moving our heads around, doing jumping jacks, running loops, and low crawling across the sand-floored building. So far so good—no leaks! Then, of course, we were told to take off our masks and once everyone had their mask off, we could walk SLOWLY out of the building. When I opened my eyes to see and took a short breath it soon became clear that tear gas was still as unpleasant as it had been the last time I did this—even more so with a sore throat! After cleaning our weapons we late comers got the opportunity to see videotaped versions of the in-briefs that we missed earlier dealing with legal, medical, insurance, pay, and other mandatory topics. Luckily the supply sergeant delivered our DCUs with nametapes and patches, so now we could change out of our BDUs that reeked of tear gas.

Barracks 5250, Old Division Area, 1030 Hours Romeo, Sunday, 18Jan2004

Today is the first rainy day since I got here, but it is warmer and a good day for rain since all we have to do today is pack and palletize our equipment to load on the C-17 Globemaster aircraft. We are told that we will be going in two flights or "chocks" and to be ready to fly by Tuesday. Now all I have to do is figure out how to cram all this gear into one rucksack, two duffle bags and a footlocker. The first duffle bag, the "A" bag holds all my TA-50 personal gear including LBE, helmet, chemical suit, gas mask, and body armor. The "B" bag holds extra clothing, uniforms, and cold weather gear. The footlocker holds goggles, books, foot powder, glasses and other crushable items. All of these are loaded onto pallets and I'm told we won't see them again until we get in country.

My bunkmate Major George Rodgers, a Baptist Minister from Mississippi, packs his footlocker prior to stacking it on a pallet for the trip to Iraq Sunday Jan 18, 2004. (DCP01907) (Photo -- Dave Conklin)

What I have left until then has to fit in my briefcase and rucksack, including my shaving kit, an extra uniform, a PT uniform, underwear, towel, books and files, a set of civilian clothes, my sleeping bag, and a folding stool. I will wear the other DCU and field jacket and carry my M16 rifle and everything else onto the plane.

Old Division Area, Fort Bragg, 1300 Hours Romeo, Monday, 19Jan2004

After the 1300 hours formation today we NCOs are given a final briefing by Command Sergeant Major Elam of the Civil Affairs and Psychological Operations Command Headquarters here at Fort Bragg. Our Combined Joint Task Force 7 (CJTF-7) will be the second rotation in Iraq. Yet CSM Elam says by the time we return, over 85% of the Army's Civil Affairs and Psychological Operations personnel will have been deployed. Where they will get enough soldiers for the next rotation is anyone's guess at this point. We are also told that we could be in country 6 months, 9 months, or a year depending on the situation. Also he says only 80% of our soldiers will be allowed to take leave while deployed, so we plan to drop names into a hat to determine who gets leave.

CSM Elam stressed NCOs doing their jobs including safety and supervision to prevent accidents as well as to prevent "stupidity." To stress the latter, he mentioned a small promotion party for an Army Specialist that quickly got out of hand in Baghdad. "How many mistakes can you spot here," CSM Elam asked. "First these soldiers change into civilian clothes. Then someone brings out some whisky he's been hiding. Another gets an AK-47 rifle he 'liberated.' Then the group 'borrows' a Humvee so they can go to the Baghdad Zoo to see Uday Hussein's man-eating rare Siberian tiger. Of course someone suggests that the guest of honor pose in front of the tiger's pen, at which time the tiger grabs him by the arm. So someone decides to shoot the tiger with the AK-47 they brought along—and of course shoots the Specialist in the arm instead of the tiger—enough said about stupidity?" the Sergeant Major asks.

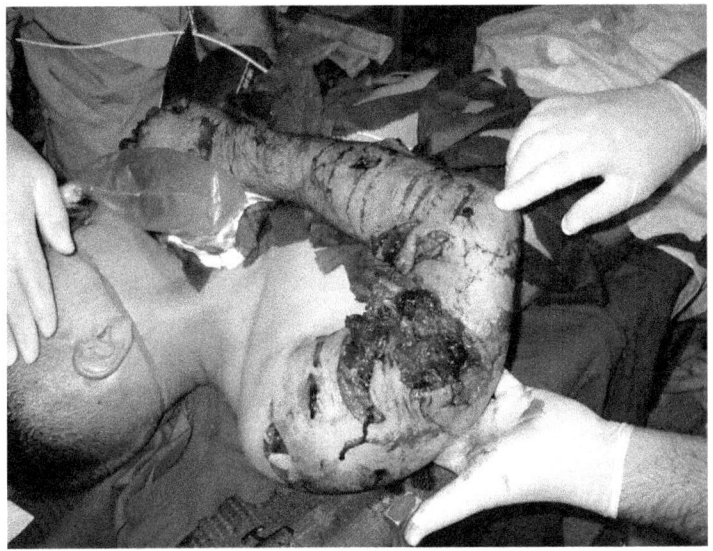

Soldier being treated at the 28th Combat Support Hospital in Baghdad for wounds inflicted by Uday Hussein's Siberian Tiger at the Baghdad Zoo Friday Sep 19, 2003. (Tiger001) (Photo -- 28th CSH)

Later in the afternoon we bring out our duffle bags and footlocker and heap them onto aluminum pallets to be strapped down with webbing, covered with plastic, and trucked over to the "green ramp" at Pope Air Force Base just a mile from our barracks. The green ramp is the loading and unloading terminal for troops and equipment being shipped out. It consists of a row of large buildings with benches and large roll-up doors that can accommodate up to 300 or so troops with full battle gear. The C17 Globemaster we will fly on is a 4-engine wide-bodied jet that holds 107 passengers or a combination of passengers and palletized baggage and equipment like our unit has. Half of our 140 troops will fly on this plane, with all of our baggage, and half will fly on another plane.

C-17 Globemaster waits on the tarmac at the end of the "Green Ramp" at Polk Air Force Base, Fayetteville, North Carolina Thursday Jan 29, 2004. (DCP01921) (Photo --Dave Conklin)

Old Division Area, Fort Bragg, 0700 Hours Romeo, Tuesday, 20Jan2004

This morning we learn that our departure has been delayed until more air transport is available—from Tuesday to maybe Saturday or later. So now the waiting begins. Back at the barracks, to be more comfortable, we hijack some seats from our rental vans and set them up in front of our bunks facing each other, with a plastic milk crate between them for a coffee table. After each meal the "Council" of seven, or nine, or however many of us are there gather to tell war stories and compare the latest equipment purchases anyone has made to "accessorize their battle rattle."

For example, our basic issue begins with 4 sets of Desert Camouflage Uniforms or "DCUs" for short. The Army will pay for sewing your nametag over the right breast pocket, U.S. Army on the left, U.S. flag on the right shoulder, and unit patch on the left. Then for $2 each we can get rank patches sewn on our collars, patrol caps, and boonie hats, and nametags in Arabic added when we get "in country." Some also get a nametag above their right rear trouser pocket as the laundry service is reported to be notorious for returning extra-large trousers to small soldiers.

Major Jeff Jurasek (left) and Lieutenant Colonel Richard Weaver, a psychologist from Florida, catch up on some reading while relaxing on the rental van seats we brought into the barracks Tuesday Jan 20, 2004.(DCP01908) (Photo --Dave Conklin)

The Army issues cold-weather gloves, but some of us bought desert camo colored Romex fire retardant gloves to use in the summer, for example when grabbing a hot rifle barrel. I also bought a $5 desert camo nylon cargo strap belt to keep my trousers up, but passed up the opportunity to get a belt-mounted baton or leg sheath and bayonet like Doc and Higgie, who I figured could be counted on to loan me theirs if need be. The DCU boots are great because they are suede and the first sergeant can't make you polish them. Since they are making shoeshine kits obsolete, in our great American entrepreneurial spirit the PX now sells DCU "boot brushing" kits.

Around our necks we wear our "dog tags" like we always have, and being in an airborne command, maybe a cross or St Michael's medal, the patron saint of paratroopers. But as this is the new hi-tech cell-phone, digital-camera, laptop-carrying Army I was also issued a computer memory stick or "thumb drive" to wear around my neck as well. My accessories also include a digital wristwatch with a 24-hour clock, date, alarm, stop and countdown watch and backlight. But I hear you can pick up a watch that also measures your "biorhythms" to help you decide which days are best to go into battle and which days to hide out.

Next is the Kevlar helmet, cloth cover, and helmet band. Most of us had our rank patch sewn on the front of the cover and last name sewn on the helmet band. Others used a marking pen on the side of the helmet band to record their favorite Psalm from the Bible; or their blood type (for some I think it was probably the only A+ grade they ever got). Then, of course, we all had Army issue goggles or a $75 pair of Wylie-X sunglasses wrapped around our helmets to look cool and occasionally to use against the sun and sand.

Officers are issued an M-9 automatic pistol, leather shoulder holster and 2 magazine pouches. But some went to the Special Ops store at Pope AFB and bought thigh holsters of desert camo colored plastic with built-in magazine pouches and rubber-coiled lanyards. Enlisted soldiers like myself are issued M16 A2 model rifles, a cleaning kit that fits in the butt plate and seven 30-round magazines. Higgie, Doc, and some of the other "Rambos" in our unit bought "mambo" slings, butt stock magazine pouches, and red-dot laser sights for their accessories. The mambo sling has a shock cord and also allows you to carry your rifle across your chest. This is great for those who need quick action and often forget where their rifle is.

The heaviest single item we wear is the Interceptor Body Armor, or IBA vest. This 20-pound flak jacket includes front and back panels for inserts that weigh 4 pounds each that can supposedly stop a 7.62mm AK-47 bullet. The load bearing equipment (LBE) mesh vest is worn over the IBA. It has 6 magazine pouches, and a belt for holding two 1-quart canteens. It also has straps and suspenders for hanging all manner of things you can get to accessorize it.

This includes but is not limited to grenades, a gas mask, flashlight, chemical light sticks, clip-on Gerber folding knife, first aid dressing pouch, earplug case, combination whistle-thermometer-compass, and a combination Rhino cell phone-Global Positioning System (GPS). If the enemy has the technology to fix your position while you're calling the nearest pizza delivery service on your Rhino, you might keep your secure frequency-hopping radio and just get a Garmin Vista GPS with a 24 megabyte memory for $279 using your on-line catalog via satellite phone downlink to your laptop. To carry enough water in the desert we are also issued a desert camo Camelback 3-liter water backpack with a zippered pouch to hold even more accessories such as our boonie hats.

To top it all off when we get to Kuwait we will be issued a basic load of 210 rounds for our M16s. So I figure that when I get dressed to go out and play in the desert each day I will weigh about 55 to 60 pounds more than I do at night. For flight manifests I have to remember to write down my weight as 200 pounds rather than 140. This, of course, doesn't include my carry bag or rucksack with sleeping bag, clothes, and folding chair — about another 40 pounds.

Barracks 5250, Old Division Area, Fort Bragg, 0900 Hours Romeo, Wednesday, 21Jan2004

We have a lot of experienced hands including a few "old timers" in their 50's like me. My cot is sandwiched between Major George Rodgers, our one-eyed Baptist minister Chaplain, and Lieutenant Colonel Richard Weaver, a psychologist from Florida. Rodgers was a Navy submariner during the Vietnam War who later joined the Army Reserve and served in Operation Desert Storm as well. He really has two eyes but one is turned inward due to a nerve injury. At the north end of the floor is Lieutenant Colonel Gamble, a railroad engineer, who at age 54 recently returned from another mission in Afghanistan last year and volunteered to go to Iraq. In the adjacent barracks is 32-year-old Specialist John "Doc" Actis, our medic. A federal drug enforcement agent and former Marine medical corpsman from Mississippi, Doc's father is a retired Navy Admiral. Doc also served in Operation Desert Storm. Next to his cot is Specialist Chad Higgenbotham. "Higgie" is a Mississippi police officer who served in Somalia with the 10th Mountain Division. He and Doc will be on the Commanding General's personal security detail or "PSD." Another veteran, Sergeant Will Perkins in the next bunk is a radio operator. "Perk" will be on the communications team or "C6." For those who don't know him, Will's disposition gives him all trappings of a serial killer, so we're happy he is on our side. Doc, Higgie, and Perk were all with the Mississippi National Guard and volunteered to deploy with the 350th.

Even though I felt comfortable going to war with these folks, I know that some of my family and one of my cousins in particular, did not:

> Subject: message from your cousin
> David, you volunteered for duty in Iraq? What the f*** is wrong with u? A righteous war would be bad enough but to put

yourself in harm's way for this ridiculous shit Bush and Cheney have conjured up is insane. Grandfathers don't volunteer for combat. Do you think u are a 20-year-old Ernest Hemingway seeking out the ultimate adventure? Has the crazed Serbian part of you taken over your soul? Please don't take any unnecessary chances, stay safe and come home healthy, so I can have the chance to kick your ass the next time I see u for putting us (all of your family) through the stress of having to worry about your crazy ass.

With Love,
Steve S

Hi Steve!
I know a lot of young people in the military here that didn't get a chance to choose, and so I figured they deserved to be led by people who aren't afraid to question stupid orders, and to question those who think it's fun to put their buddies at risk every day for no reason. I hope I can make some sense out of why the U.S. thinks it needs to occupy the center of the Arab world -- and, of course, there's this crazy Serbian side of me. . .

Cousin Dave

Pope Air Force Base, North Carolina, 1400 Hours Romeo, Thursday, 29Jan2004

This is our third bus trip this week to the passenger terminal or "Green Ramp" at Pope Air Force Base. The first chock of 30 left last Saturday, but our second chock of 47 hasn't been so lucky. Twice before we packed our rucks and duffle bags and waited 4 to 6 hours for flights that were either cancelled due to ice storms or overweight from other units bringing extra bags. This time we are told that a chartered "Omni Air International" DC-10 will pick up a transportation company at Fort Benning, then stop here for us this evening. We stand in line to swipe our military ID cards for the flight manifest as do 52 soldiers from the 44th Medical Command's 257th Medical Company, an active duty dental unit going to Iraq via Kuwait also.

After another 6-hour wait we are happy to hear that the plane has landed. Without bags, our group tips the scale at 10,340 pounds and there are plenty of seats on the plane—I get 3 of them. We put our M16s on the floor and fly all night to Ramstein Air Base in Germany where we stop at

1100 hours to refuel. We are airborne again shortly after noon—destination Southwest Asia.

A 350th Civil Affairs Soldier catches up on some reading during the 9-hour wait for our flight at the "Green Ramp" at Pope Air Force Base near Fort Bragg, North Carolina Thursday Jan 29, 2004. (DCP01922) (Photo --Dave Conklin)

2. On to Kuwait

Somewhere over Iraq, 2000 Hours Charlie, Friday, 30Jan2004

An eerie sight greeted my tired eyes as I looked out of the window of the plane. In the darkness thirty thousand feet below I could see a dozen or so scattered fires burning brightly. I knew we must be over Iraq now because these were oil-processing plants burning off excess natural gas. Here and there also were a few scattered lights from small towns and villages. Finally after 16 hours in the air and crossing 8 time zones since we left Fort Bragg we were going to land soon. We flew out over the Persian Gulf and Kuwait City before making a wide turn on our final approach to Al Jaber Air Base.

The air had a strangely sweet smell and the temperature was a mild 50 F as I walked in the darkness to the bus waiting to take us to Camp Wolverine. The Combined Forces Land Component Command (CFLCC) here under LTG McKiernan also includes Camp Arifjan, Doha, Virginia, Wolf, Ali Al-Sembi Air Base, and farthest away, Camp Udairi. We are led to a briefing tent where we all swiped our military ID cards so that finance can start our hostile fire pay, hardship pay, and separate rations. Then we sit on benches for the briefing that covers safety (again), finance, and rules of engagement.

Signs point the way to the briefing tent at Camp Wolverine near Al Jaber Air Base, Kuwait City, Kuwait Friday Jan 30, 2004. (DCP01927) (Photo --Dave Conklin)

Some of our unit will be stationed in Kuwait at Camp Arifjan or Doha, while most of us will go on to Iraq to join LTG Sanchez's Combined

Joint Task Force 7 (CJTF-7). Still under construction, Camp Wolverine's purpose is to process troops and send them on to other staging area camps. Until our MP escort arrives, we have time to get a midnight dinner at the dining facility or DFAC (dee-fack) as the Army calls it, and shop at the PX which is open 24/7.

As we board the bus for the four-hour ride to Camp Udairi we are each issued 20 rounds of ammunition, which is not very helpful considering we had taken the bolts out of our rifles as required by the Air Force and all of our magazines were packed. As we left the air base, we passed a highway sign in Arabic. "Look," I said, "It says Welcome to Kuwait City, Home of the World Champion Braves." "Really?" someone asked. I replied, "No you idiot. I can't read Arabic!"

Camp Udairi, Kuwait, 0900 Hours Charlie, Saturday, 31Jan2004

The sun was rising by the time our bus and military police escort left the paved road and continued on the washboard gravel and sand road past Ali Al-Salam Air Base to Camp Udairi. The camp is a staging area for troops and convoys going to Iraq. It is only about 30 kilometers from the Iraqi border and surrounded by nothing but sand and a few camel and goat herders. The tallest landmark for 50 kilometers was the unfinished water tower in the center of camp next to the only paved road near which someone put a street sign that said "Eisenhower Drive."

The bus dropped us at Tent 4, Pad 6A, one of the hundreds of 30 by 100 foot tents made in Pakistan and pitched over a wood frame floor with 60 cots and about a dozen heater/air conditioner units scattered along the walls. Outside the tent was a pallet of boxes filled with 1-liter bottles of water and a large diesel generator to power the fluorescent lights and heaters of several tents. Also outside was a row of porta-potties and three shower trailers. A half-mile back down the road was the dining facility, in one of the few temporary plastic buildings in this huge tent city.

The whole place looked like the first scene of the movie MASH with troops everywhere. One dusty Humvee and 5-ton truck convoy from the 101st Airborne Division just arrived from the two-day trip from Baghdad to redeploy back to the states after a long hard year, while the 29th Signal Battalion in the next row of tents loaded up to replace other battle-worn soldiers. Soon 12,000 troops would fill this camp as part of the largest troop rotation since the end of World War II.

Looking South along Eisenhower Drive over Camp Udairi, Kuwait, built as a division-sized staging area for U.S. Army troops deploying to Operation Iraqi Freedom Sunday Feb 1, 2004. (DCP01932) (Photo --Dave Conklin)

We dug out our sleeping bags and slept, weary after our 2-day trip from the states. That evening, we met up with the rest of our unit that arrived 5 days earlier. Each of us received two bullet-proof slates for our IBA (Interceptor body armor), three atropine injectors to carry as a nerve gas antidote, 200 rounds of ammunition, and a self-adjusting tourniquet for our first aid kit. Still reeling from lack of sleep and crossing 8 time zones, I fell asleep despite the constant "ron-ron-ron" of the diesel generator outside the tent.

Tent 4, Pad 6A, Camp Udairi, 0600 Hours Charlie, Sunday, 1Feb2004

"Wake up Sergeant Schumate! Yes, you're still here," hollered Command Sergeant Major Jim Maree to the guy next to me. "Click your heels three times and see if that helps any." I seriously doubted that it would as I dressed and grabbed my M16, helmet and body armor for the half-mile hike to the chow hall with Major Rodgers.

Having been in the Gulf War thirteen years earlier, Rodgers said the only improvement he saw in the Army camps was the chow. The dining facility was now in a temporary building rather than a tent, and Filipinos and Pakistanis hired by contractors were doing the serving rather than soldiers. He said the food was better with fresh fruit and pop machines as well as a short order line. But I was having flashbacks to the 1870s as I ate my cold cereal, boxed milk, coffee, and a biscuit that looked and tasted exactly like hardtack, except for the yeast that made it rise. Tomorrow I think I will try the French toast, sausage patties and scrambled eggs.

Lunch today in the four main lines is beef stew, salad or canned corn, bread, jello, and apple, pear or banana juice in a box, or coffee, milk or soda pop. Dinner is pretty much the same or you can have a hamburger, pizza or lasagna in the two short order lines.

I was happy to get three hot meals a day but the quality and variety decreased as we got farther away from Kuwait City. We always had a case of Meals Ready to Eat (MREs) nearby just in case, but we only ate them when we were on the move. Even though they have improved over the years, our local nickname for them was "Meals Rejected by Ethiopians."

Home sweet home for 60 of us at Tent 4, Pad 6A, Camp Udairi, Kuwait staging area for the 350th Civil Affairs Command as we deploy to Operation Iraqi Freedom Sunday Feb 1, 2004. (DCP01934) (Photo --Dave Conklin)

The Tactical Operations Center or "TOC" for III Corps at Camp Udairi, Kuwait staging area Sunday Feb 1, 2004. (DCP01931) (Photo --Dave Conklin)

Third Corps Tactical Operations Center, Camp Udairi, 1300 Hours Charlie, Monday, 2Feb2004

I was told that we might have to drive ourselves to the rifle range so they arranged for us to get a driver's license. Only eight of us volunteered for drivers training, however 40 soldiers from several units were waiting when the staff sergeant in charge arrived to train and test us for our Non Tactical Vehicle (NTV) license to drive cars and buses in Kuwait and Iraq. He showed us Xerox copies of the road signs, told us the speed limits (30km per hour max on the camp main road), and gave us the telephone number to report accidents as if any of us had a phone, let alone a car.

Then, since he had only ten tests, in typical Army fashion we were told to break into groups of four each and write the group's answer to each question on a piece of paper with all of our names on it. We would get a group grade and if we passed, a license. I wondered if this meant that all four of us would have to drive the bus at the same time too!

That night I was tasked to give a welcome brief to two more of our incoming battalions to include: that the use of bottled water is necessary for drinking and brushing your teeth; that the laundry tent takes four days to clean your uniforms; that weapons status is green (not loaded) with muzzle pointed down in camp; that you keep your tent lines taut so the rain and wind won't get in; and that phone calls to the states cost $1 per minute. After my last brief a soldier walked up to me in the darkness and says, "Remember when they shut down our plane engine last summer on our way back from Osan, Korea?" It turns out to be my old friend Major Guiles from the 425th Civil Affairs Battalion in Santa Barbara, California. It's a small world when you're in the Army.

Camp Udairi Airfield, 0800 Hours Charlie, Tuesday, 3Feb2004

Most of us are already getting bored waiting to move on to Iraq, so LTC Parrish, our flight surgeon lines up a CH-47 Chinook helicopter and 16 of us volunteer for medical evacuation or "medevac" training in the desert this morning. The CH-47 is the workhorse of the helicopter set and can carry people, cargo, or sling load an artillery piece if need be. The Chinook crew has been in Iraq for eight months and is hoping to rotate back to the states in a month or so. They tell me they can carry up to 24 litters of patients at a time on 6 racks of 4 each. Before we even start the helicopter we rig the chopper up for a rack of 4 and practice with 4 people in full combat gear carrying an empty litter to the top rack and then a full litter.

Finally the first group of eight of us fly off under sunny skies in a light breeze and 50 F temperatures into the Kuwaiti desert over Bedouin sheep and goat herds, old dozer berms, and terrain pockmarked with tank fighting positions from the 1991 Gulf War. We leave the back ramp open for the view and land just past a herd of 30 camels on land so flat you would swear that a giant bulldozer had smoothed out the wrinkles a millennium ago. Now it was our chance to try our hands at carrying litters off of the helo while the blades are turning and the dust is blowing. After we "de-littered" the aircraft, it flew back to the airfield for the next group.

Specialist John Actis, 350th Civil Affairs Command Medic, sprints out of a CH-47 Chinook helicopter with a stretcher in one hand and an M16 rifle in the other during a "hot" landing exercise in the Kuwaiti desert near the border of Iraq Tuesday Feb 3, 2004. (DCP01938) (Photo --Dave Conklin)

Staff Sergeant Dave Conklin (front right) and soldiers from the 350th Civil Affairs Command in full combat gear in the Kuwaiti desert near Camp Udairi Tuesday Feb 3, 2004. (DCP01939) (Photo -- Dave Conklin)

The only signs of life on this empty plain were a few sprigs of green grass where the goats haven't been lately, and an occasional dragonfly. While we were preparing our "patients" for the helo's return I found some rusty chunks of twisted metal, probably from Saddam's Army's last retreat from Kuwait. After about 20 minutes the Chinook returned and landed about 50 yards away. We sprinted with our litter patients back onto the bird and were back at camp in time for lunch.

Right after lunch I was told to pack and be ready to fly to Baghdad by 1600 hours. . . at 1700 hours I finally decided to go have dinner. . . at 1800 hours we were told to move our duffle bags across the road to another tent. . . and finally at 1900 hours we were told to get some rest as the buses wouldn't be here to take us to the airplane until 0300 hours.

28   *An Iraq War Diary*

Ali Al-Sembi Air Base, Kuwait, 0600 Hours Charlie, Wednesday, 4Feb2004

Our bus driver was Staff Sergeant Mayer, about the only guy who didn't take the driving test. We finally got into the Air Base after waking

Most of us from the 350th Civil Affairs Command are happy to be on the first "chock" of 30 soldiers and palletized baggage. We strap in for a C-130 Hercules flight from Ali Al-Sembi Air Base in Kuwait to Baghdad, Iraq. Wednesday Feb 4, 2004. (DCP01943) (Photo --Dave Conklin)

up the gate guards. As we approached the tarmac, we could see that the French-built airplane bunkers still had neat holes in the top or side where smart bombs had destroyed Saddam Hussein's air force after his brief conquest of Kuwait in 1991. We piled our duffle bags on two pallets and loaded them and us on the C-130 Hercules cargo plane. Soon we taxied past the Specter AC-130 gunships on the tarmac and finally took off into the sun, over Kuwait City, over the Persian Gulf, turning north to follow the Tigris and Euphrates Rivers to Baghdad.

3. Welcome to Baghdad

Over Baghdad International Airport, 1025 Hours Charlie, Wednesday, 4Feb2004

As we approached the western outskirts of Baghdad our pilot began a series of tight turns followed by a steep dive and dropping chaff flares to evade possible surface-to-air fire as our C-130 Hercules cargo plane made a combat landing at Baghdad International, known as BIAP (Bye-App) by the troops here. What we didn't know was that BIAP was closed earlier this morning after 3 rocket attacks and was just reopened as we arrived. It had been raining recently but the sky was clear and sunny this morning and the temperature stood at 60 F as we walked off the plane and over to the muddy parking lot where our pallets of duffle bags were dropped.

Bombed out Ba'ath Party Headquarters near the Presidential Palace in the Green Zone, Baghdad Friday Feb 13, 2004. (DCP01978) (Photo --Dave Conklin)

Since the 10 miles or so from the airport to our destination in the "Green Zone" was not a secure area, we were required to wear helmets and body armor and have our weapons locked and loaded. My first impression of the highway into Baghdad was that it looked pretty much the same as it did when I saw it on the six o'clock news last April when U.S. troops first arrived. Convoys of M-2 Bradley Fighting Vehicles and Humvees traveled back and forth on the highway lined by date palms while Iraqis in small cars and Toyota pickups weaved in and out of the traffic lanes. Since April the underbrush, small trees, and abandoned vehicles have all been hauled off so that they could not be used to hide explosives. Iraqi policemen with AK-47 rifles guarded each overpass so that bombs could not be dropped onto convoys from above.

We passed through one of the 6 checkpoints into the Green Zone where the Civilian Provisional Authority or CPA offices are as well as a number of Army command headquarters. We passed by dirty streets, cracked sidewalks, broken streetlights, and trash scattered by the wind. Yet just behind, in stark contrast, stood the monumental ministry buildings and palaces built by Saddam Hussein. Other than the bomb damage to some of the buildings, Baghdad reminded me a lot of Bucharest and other cities I saw in Eastern Europe during the 1990s after the demise of socialism had left them decrepit and in disrepair, after their dictators had drained the wealth of the country for their own aggrandizement.

Palace of the King of Jordan, Green Zone, Baghdad, 1100 Hours Charlie, Thursday, 5Feb2004

Baghdad may be a war zone and a dangerous place for an American in uniform, but compared to our tent camp in the Kuwaiti desert, at first glance this is a paradise compared to that. For the Civil Affairs Command Tactical Operations Center or "TOC" we confiscated the Palace that Saddam built on the west bank of the Tigris River for visits by the King of Jordan. Large ornate doors, marble floors, and gold-plated bathroom fixtures all attest to his extravagance.

Second floor sinks in the Palace of the King of Jordan, Baghdad Thursday Feb 12, 2004. (DCP01956) (Photo --Dave Conklin)

The balcony outside our third floor office looks eastward across the turbid Tigris with downtown Baghdad and the Sheraton Hotel in center view. Behind the Sheraton I can see the Shahid Mosque that the news media use as a backdrop when they broadcast from the hotel's balcony. To the west of our palace in the immediate compound is a grassy park with duck ponds, waterfalls, citrus trees and date palms. Nearby are former vacation residences of Saddam's relatives and party members.

We are constantly reminded of the war by the pair of security helicopters with heavily armed men hanging out of them constantly swooping up and down the river trying to draw fire from anyone stupid enough to shoot at them. I could list a lot of other distractions from the splendor of what at first appears to be an expensive resort. Included on this list would be the constant drone of the generators that keep the power on: the radio, telephone, and computer wires climbing up the side of our building like kudzu vines; the armed Gurkha guards at the concrete barrier checkpoints; and of course the bullet holes in the wall above my desk in the G8 (finance section).

Green Zone, Baghdad, Iraq, 1145 Hours Charlie, Monday, 9Feb2004

Nothing much new to report except that I have a colonel who wants me to be his public affairs action officer for the civil affairs command, a major that already has me working as our liaison officer for purchasing and contracting, and a Navy commander in the Joint Contracting Office who wants me to be his purchasing agent. I'll let them fight it out I guess. Today four of us went to the airport to pick up our mail and visit the PX. It's only a 10-mile trip but we are required to have at least four people and two-vehicles. By the way, the Baghdad Expressway is better known today as "Route Irish," and it is arguably the most dangerous highway in the world. We go to "weapons red" status outside the Green Zone, meaning that we lock and load our pistols and rifles and wear full body armor due to the potential for ambushes and homemade improvised explosive devices, or "IEDs" along the way.

Staff Sergeant Sean Sullivan is one of our drivers today. "Sully" is an ex-cop from Massachusetts and a Russian linguist Kosovo veteran. He arrived in Iraq for the war and later trained Iraqi police officers with the 422nd Civil Affairs Battalion west of Baghdad in Fallujah until last July. Now he's a liaison to contracting until his unit rotates out in mid-March. The driver usually tries to find a short gun to carry on his lap rather than have none at all. Sully has a confiscated MP-5 9mm German-made submachine gun and drives like Will Smith on the chase scene in the movie "Bad Boys 2."

Staff Sergeant Sean Sullivan drives our Toyota Land Cruiser while I ride "shotgun" in heavy traffic on Route Irish March 14, 2004. (DCP02065) (Photo --Dave Conklin)

At 150 kilometers per hour, we figure we can be past an explosive device before it can be triggered. Unfortunately, the local traffic is traveling about half that speed, so reaction time is minimal. Last December four of my friends in the 372nd Mobile Public Affairs Unit were seriously injured when their Humvee rolled after clipping a truck that squeezed them out.

By the way, our four office vehicles are NTVs (non-tactical vehicles). These SUVs (sport utility vehicles) are two white Nissan Pathfinders and two white Toyota Land Cruisers that were confiscated from Usay and Uday Hussein's garage last spring. We had 5 SUV's before one was destroyed in a rocket attack, but that's another story.

After we returned from the mail run, a Captain from the 1st Armored Division dropped by to check on a contract. He had an Egyptian made AK-47 rifle and a bag full of 7.62mm ammunition that his guys took off an Iraqi on the way here. Since the Captain didn't need any more A-Ks, he asked if we wanted it--so we added it to our weapons stash. A Kalashnikov or "A-K" here goes for about $25 and there are a lot of them around.

Al Rasheed Hotel, Green Zone, Baghdad, 0725 Hours Charlie, Wednesday, 11Feb2004

A loud CRACK split the air, followed by a rising cloud of dust somewhere behind the concrete wall in front of us. Staff Sergeant

Pangelinan and I were clearing our weapons at the checkpoint outside the Al Rasheed Hotel as a light rain began to fall. It was definitely an explosion of some kind and since I didn't hear the whistling sound of a mortar shell and no follow-up strike, I was afraid that it might be another IED or "Improvised Explosive Device" set by a terrorist.

It wasn't long before my fears were confirmed. When we got back to the Contracting Office the Field Ordering Officers were coming in for their weekly clearing. They had the TV tuned to CNN and were watching a reporter standing in the rain at the bombsite. Apparently a suicide attacker driving a white 1991 Oldsmobile Cutlass Sierra detonated about 300 to 500 pounds of explosives in a crowd of hundreds of Iraqis waiting outside a nearby Baghdad army recruiting center, killing 46 people in the second bombing in two days targeting Iraqis working with the U.S.-led coalition. Yesterday a suicide bombing against a police station south of the capital killed 53 people.

Locations of recent suicide attacks in Iraq Feb 11, 2004. (Map/ AFP)

We had heard that insurgents would step up violence to disrupt the planned June 30 handover of power to the Iraqis. It looked like they were making good on a promise by Jordanian militant Abu Musab Al Zarqawi to spark a Sunni-Shiite civil war in a last-ditch attempt to wreck the handover. American cars like the one used in the attack are popular in Jordan. Our command is sending a team to Jordan to work with Iraqis there also.

The rain had stopped by noon, and I was back at the Convention Center across from the Al Rasheed Hotel again, this time to visit the Coalition Press Information Center where one of my Army photojournalist schoolmates Sergeant Tyrone Walker was working. I could see Tyrone was battle-weary and ready to go home. His unit was due to rotate out in a week. He had volunteered for the operation in

Afghanistan in 2001, only to return to South Carolina where his unit was activated again for the war in Iraq.

Cars engulfed in flames after suicide bomb attack Monday, Dec 15, 2003. (DSCI0027) (Photo -- 372 MPAD)

Home of Mohammad Al-Neamy, Baghdad, 2030 Hours Charlie, Thursday, 12Feb2004

One of our Iraqi interpreters, twenty-three year old Shama Al Neamy, one of four sisters in this extended family of 17 had invited us to have a traditional Iraqi dinner and evening with her family. Five of us from the Joint Contracting Office arrived for dinner at about 6 o'clock and parked our Toyota inside the gated driveway to the modest Al-Neamy house. The patriarch was her 70-year old grandfather. When I asked Shama what his name was, she replied, "Mohammed." I felt a little embarrassed, having a 20 percent chance of guessing it myself. It seemed to me that every fifth Muslim male I met was named "Mohammed," the other four being Ahkmed, Abdulla, Hassan, and Omar.

Mohammed also *looked* like an Arab. He was dressed in the traditional Iraqi black-and-white checkered headscarf, a dark *jalabeeya* robe and sandals. As I watched him loosely twirl his prayer beads in his right hand I noticed an ornate tattoo that disappeared into the sleeve of the *jalabeeya*. His large chiseled nose, brown eyes, skin and hair, thick mustache and eyebrows had obviously been passed down to the rest of his family. When he smiled at my translated jokes his upper-left gold-capped canine tooth gleamed, but his right canine was missing.

Like many Iraqis, Mohammed said he had been a farmer, and like many Muslims, had made the pilgrimage to the *Haj* in the holy city of

Mecca where his prophet namesake was born. This earned him the right to be known as *"Hajji"* Mohammed. As if on cue, his grandson Kusay brought in a *djadja* or chicken from the back yard and a flat of brown eggs from the kitchen. So I told them that my family also has chickens that lay brown eggs and *green* eggs as well! After Shama translated this, there was much discussion in Arabic and disbelief that a chicken could lay a green egg! I explained that they were a breed known as Araucana and that only the shell was green, not the inside.

The conversation got around to Iraq's economy—or lack thereof. Mohammed's son Talib felt that the best years he knew were during the 1970s when Iraq was a republic and oil sales from newly developed oil fields began to enrich the country. The British had gone, the Kings were overthrown, and Saddam Hussein was yet to take over and start costly wars with his neighbors. Talib said bribery was rampant under Saddam. He said for example, police officers made the equivalent of $5 per week and it was so easy to bribe them with a pack of cigarettes that emphysema from smoking became known as "police lung."

Seventy year-old Mohammed Al Neamy, (center), his wife (front), and son Talib (right) and family enjoy inviting friends to dinner in their Baghdad home, Thursday Feb 12, 2004.
(DCP01968) (Photo --Dave Conklin)

Dinner was served in the traditional way, which meant that only men were allowed at the table. Shama was only allowed to eat with us because she was translating. She sat down last, next to Mohammed. The meal was delicious and included flat bread, rolls, lamb kebab, mixed vegetables with rice, and baked chicken halves. No alcohol was served at any time during the evening, only thick sludgy Arabian coffee before dinner, water and Pepsi Cola with dinner, and hot sweet tea seasoned with cardamom after dinner. What I didn't know until later was that only after our dinner were the women and children allowed to eat—whatever they took off the table back to the kitchen. Soon the lights went out as the power grid in this war-torn city shut down for the night. Our flashlights and lanterns came out as we bid farewell to the Al Neamy family and drove back down the deserted street to the Green Zone and our own compound.

Former Security Police Residence, Green Zone, 1000 Hours Charlie, Friday, 13Feb2004

The Joint Contracting and Finance Office is a four-story building located on Haifa Street in central Baghdad just south of Ibn Sina Hospital in the International Zone (Green Zone). It is the former security police residence and compound. The Joint Contracting Office is on the ground floor. I have a desk here where we write and monitor the contracts for supplies, materials, and projects. The Joint Finance Office is on the second floor. These are the folks that cash the checks and pay the bills including paying for completed projects. On the third and fourth floors are our sleeping quarters, usually two bunks per room. I got lucky and did not have a roommate as no one wanted my room on the third floor after it was hit by a rocket that injured the soldier who had it just before me. The roof is accessible by stairs and is where we set up a weight-room and had room for gatherings, promotions, holiday parties, and just stargazing.

Even though I belonged to the 350th Civil Affairs Command, I was embedded with the Contracting Office so that my command could use me to write their priority contracts and also because they were short of bunks. One day per week I work at the civil affairs HQ as their finance NCO inputting budgets and expenditures into the Army finance system and keeping them from overspending.

Once a week a car would drive into the compound and two men with duffle bags and an armed guard would get out and go up to the finance office. I found out later that they delivered about $1 million per week to finance so they could pay all the creditors. I also saw contractors come down from finance with duffle bags and I am sure they were full of cash. Once I was shown the safe where the cash was kept until it was needed. I thought, "If I had a million dollars in 100s, could I carry that much?" Well

I found out that I could indeed carry that much, but not away from that room.

Staff Sergeant Dave Conklin poses with two bricks of $100,000 each from the Joint Finance Office safe Feb 18, 2004. (QSZQE6219) (Photo --Dave Conklin)

Baghdad, 1130 Hours Charlie, Sunday, 15Feb2004

Today began clear, cool, and windy but by noon a rust-colored fog blew in from the northwest and enveloped the city. But this wasn't a fog, it was dust and it coated everything including the floors inside the buildings. It was the first sandstorm of the *shamal* or *haboob* desert sandstorm season.

U.S. troops pass under the gate near the Presidential Palace in Baghdad in the rusty haze of a desert sandstorm Sunday Feb 15, 2004. (DCP01980) (Photo --Dave Conklin)

Gunman on Baghdad's Matar Saddam al-Dowli Expressway, better known as "Route Irish," near Camp Victory Friday Feb 13, 2004. (DCP01971) (Photo --Dave Conklin)

The spring storms roll across the desert churning up giant dust clouds and reducing visibility to practically nothing. The storms come with changes in the weather, like the 12 inches of snow Amman, Jordan woke up to this morning. By sunset, the dust had dissipated as fast as it arrived.

Ba Qubah, 1130 Hours Charlie, Monday, 16Feb2004

As I was walking past the hospital I could see the Blackhawk medevac chopper come in for a landing, and then disappear into the courtyard behind. It was only later I learned that today would see the first death of one of our own civil affairs soldiers who just arrived with us in country this month.

This evening at chow Major Earnest, our G1 (personnel officer), explained that a soldier from the 415th Civil Affairs Battalion attached to Task Force Iron Horse was killed and four others were seriously wounded when a 152mm artillery shell made into a bomb exploded in the highway median at about 9:40 a.m. in the center of Ba Qubah, about 35 miles northeast of Baghdad. The young female PFC was the driver of the last Humvee of a 5-vehicle convoy and was literally blown to pieces. From what I have seen, many convoys go too slow and the army trucks and Humvees are too close together. We take only two unmarked SUVs when possible and try to get past danger before it can happen. According to the media, the attacks against our troops here in February have increased to between 20 and 24 a day, rising from 18 per day in January.

My retired Navy submariner friend from Maine writes:

> Dave:
> I guess our 20 below zero weather in Northern Maine beats sandstorms. We're enjoying the grandchildren here on Presidents' Day. Rod Sirois and his community have a power struggle going on with the U.S. Customs there at the St. Pamphile border. Fun and games! The Fox News Channel carried an interview with Rod and a poor old timer who is to be charged $10,000 for going to church. I've been trying to catch the video. My uncle in Utah has seen it twice.
>
> I suspect Rod has advised you of the upcoming referendum on bear baiting, trapping, and running with dogs. This next season may be our last. Rod said COL Sam may be back for this season. I'll be guiding with Rod for the second year. I did this for two weeks last season. It's a lot of fun. I really learned a lot working with Rod and Dan Glidden. Right now I'm reading Ollie North's book WAR STORIES regarding the Iraqi War. I've also read HUNTING FOR BIN LADEN to learn more about the situation. And I thought the problem was complex when I was active.
>
> It looks like this next election is going to be a street fight. It's too bad we've lost the high road and all sense of dignity. There's no such thing as real history anymore; it's what the spin doctors and prevaricators feed to us. Maybe I'm naive and it's always been like that.
>
> Bobby Reed, my partner on the "Brothers of the Dolphin" music album is breathing easier these days. His son was in the 101st [Airborne Division], mostly around Mosul, and just got back to Fort Campbell. They saw a lot of action. His group was backup for the guys who captured the rat in the hole. It's been a long year for the Reeds.
>
> We are enjoying retirement. Although the monthly income exceeds our long-term goals from years ago, it seems we're still 20% short of what we need. You wouldn't believe how many are lined up to get that amount away from us. In 1960 when I was in boot camp I received my first lifer lecture.

I never forgot the terms. The instructor advised that most of us who did 20 years would probably retire as an E-7 [Master Chief], make $127 per month, get full medical coverage, and never have to work again. What a deal! Thought you'd get a kick out of that. Hope all is going well with you. Will look forward to your e-mails. Thank you for that. We pray for your safety.

Tommy

San Francisco, California, 2320 Hours Sierra, Tuesday, 17Feb2004
My friend Alison Hayden in San Francisco writes:

Thanks Dave, for taking the time to journal and to include me on the circular. It's a great assurance to know that we have such men in our armed forces. I thank you for doing your duty with what I know is your whole heart and mind. Although wholly objective, the photos and your words behold a chilling sobriety on which I dare not to ruminate. There's a foreboding in my gut about what lies ahead for us all, in Iraq and in our country. While you and the many valiant soldiers risk their lives in such places, there are some very frightening changes taking place back home of which I'm sure you're aware. We are at crucial juncture in eradicating what made and protects this country at its core: the allegiance to God's sovereignty and justice, as every reference is sought to be stripped from essential defining documents of our nation and its courthouse walls; the protection and sanctity of the sacrament of marriage, a sure death to the family unit.

Alison

Baghdad, Iraq, 1815 Hours Charlie, Friday, 20Feb2004
Besides writing and sending my journal stories to concerned friends, I also write letters home as much as I can.

Dear Mary:
I got your green egg and Araucana chicken photos today. Thanks. The Iraqis didn't believe we had chickens that lay green eggs. Glad things are quiet at home. Things have been quiet here too for the last few days (which means only sporadic gunfire, but no "nearby" mortar or rocket attacks). Friday is the Muslim

"weekend" and most offices are closed but soldiers and Iraqi vendors still come in with questions and phone calls, and we are pretty much trapped here in the Green Zone where it is "safe" unless we go in a convoy. I wanted to tell you that I use the collapsible metal cup you gave me at least three times a day and always read your inscription [Remember we love you]. I hope the photos come out OK with the stories I send back. Let me know if they don't or if they take too long to download.

The job that I'm doing right now, that of being a resource manager (Contracting and Finance) for the 350th, is not real exciting, but important to the overall effort. I'm sure you'll be glad to know that it seems to be one of the safer jobs here as well as having some of the best living accommodations. For example, Jeff, one of the Air Force tech sergeants here didn't like his bed so he talked the commander into ordering new mattresses for all of us by including them in a mattress contract he is doing. But I am anxious to see the city and the countryside where the Iraqi people live, even if that is where the convoys are being ambushed. But there is time for this later I think.

Love, Dave

When I find a postcard I often write home with a pen instead of a computer and the postage is free. Sunday, Feb 22, 2004. (Photo --Dave Conklin)

Baghdad, Iraq, 2215 Hours Charlie, Sunday, 22Feb2004

Dear Mary,

Thanks for the newsy e-mail. Thanks for the jokes and the soldier photos too! I should be taking some of those shots. I wish I had more time for that, but I am still busy trying to learn as much as I can about my current job.

I had a great day yesterday after our trip to the airport to take one of our departing Air Force guys to catch a plane home (they only stay for a 90-120 day rotation). Anyway there was a box waiting for me here at the unit HQ from my honey--full of books! It was sent on Feb 9 and got here about Feb 19 (only 10 days) but I got it yesterday as they only check the mail every few days. Thanks a lot!

By the way, the latest rumor (remember, these are all just rumors) is that we will be home by October . . . BUT the rest of the rumor is that's because the Army will send us to Afghanistan 90 days later and with the Army's stop loss program, we won't be able to quit or join a different unit. But remember this is just the latest rumor!

Love, Dave

CPA Parking Lot, Green Zone, 1900 Hours Charlie, Friday, 27Feb2004

I had heard there was a "Hash" in Baghdad. Now I had proof. I try to work out at least three times per week whenever and wherever I can. Friday I was running past the CPA parking lot on an evening run when I saw a group of about 20 people spray painting a circle on the concrete with a cross in it and a letter in each quarter: B-H-H-H for the "free Baghdad Hash House Harriers." The hash is an informal, multinational and VERY laid back "running and drinking club" that has chapters in almost every major city in the world. I was told it began with a couple of Spaniards in 1939 who had such a bad dish of hash in Kuala Lumpur that they agreed to run off the grease, and then drink until they forgot all about the bad meal. These days many chapters of the Hash House Harriers even have websites.

As a former member of the Sofia, Bulgaria Hash I decided I would join the group for a run and a free beer at the end—especially the beer since none was to be had or consumed through official channels. This was to be the 39th week of the Baghdad Hash since the war. The hares lead the way setting the trail and checkpoints with the bugler following behind.

But this was one of the most unusual hashes I have ever run. First of all, Baghdad is a combat zone. Rockets, mortars, and machine gun fire are not all that uncommon, even in the "Green Zone." Secondly, we were running at night, in the dark, without streetlights most of the way. I also noticed that the "trail markers" were not made from flour, but were little piles of shredded paper from document shredders. Finally, the trail went through bombed-out buildings, war rubble, and checkpoints with armed guards.

As I ran past the machine gun nests in front of the CPA Presidential Palace shouting "ON, ON" I could hear helicopters on patrol whizzing past at treetop height. Soon we backtracked down a dark alley, through backyards, across the main street, under the 14 July Bridge, and through the motor pool. We passed Gurkhas with M16s and private guards with AK-47s, and MP-5s. I wondered if anyone would get trigger-happy tonight. We ran on sidewalks, jumping over open manholes. We ran in the street dodging Bradley fighting vehicles, over rubble, spike strips, down narrow alleys, and through cracks between barrier walls. I tried to follow runners who had headlamps but still managed to trip over a fallen lamppost and fall on my face.

A Baghdad hasher finds the trail through a hole in the wall made by a tank round during the evening run Friday, Feb 27, 2004 (IMG_008) (Photo -- Will Merrill)

The Hash Circle anoints "Al Zheimer" into their group after an evening run Friday, Feb 27, 2004. (IMG_011) (Photo -- Will Merrill)

Forty-five minutes and a few bruises later I came to a "B-N" marked on the pavement with shredded paper. The initials for "Beer Near" meant that the end would have been in sight if it weren't so dark. We gathered at a pumping station on the north bank of the Tigris River. The city of Baghdad bustled on the other side. The constellation of Orion was visible high above the city. As sporadic gunfire cracked in the night, I thought it would be best if I didn't stand too close to anyone who had a headlamp on. The evening went rather well up until the point where I was called to the center of the circle to guzzle a large can of Heineken for forgetting my hash name. More beer was then poured over my head as I knelt down for the anointment of my new hash name—"Al Zheimer." The forgetful one.

4. Baghdad Winter

Kazimiya Shrine, Baghdad, 1000 Hours Charlie, Tuesday, 02Mar2004

By now I have learned that wherever there are crowds here, there is danger. Sure enough, during the day I heard the muffled simultaneous explosions that ripped through crowds of worshippers at Shiite Muslim shrines across the river from us in Baghdad, and I heard that Karbala was hit also, killing at least 143 people on the holiest day of the Shiite calendar. The newspapers said it was the bloodiest day since the end of major fighting. Our translators Nibras and Suhad were both given the day off, even though it is a religious holiday only for Shiites. Nibras is a Shiite Muslim but said she would stay at home. The next morning they both had a long wait in line to get past the checkpoint so they could come to work.

The Ashoura festival marks the 7th century killing of Imam Hussein. It is the most important religious period in Shiite Islam and draws hundreds of thousands of pilgrims from Iraq, Iran, Pakistan and other Shiite communities to the Iraqi shrines. Imam Hussein, a grandson of the prophet Muhammad, is buried in Karbala and the blasts there occurred near the golden-domed shrine that contains his tomb. The Kazimiya shrine here in northern Baghdad contains the tombs of two other Shiite saints, Imam Mousa Kazem and his grandson Imam Muhammad al-Jawad.

Imam Hussein, killed in a power struggle in 680, is buried in a gold-domed shrine in Karbala. His death was part of a dispute over leadership of the faith. It was also a key event in Islam's split into the Sunni and Shiite branches. As reported by the media here, this is the first time in a generation that Iraq's Shiites have been free to publicly celebrate the holiday. "We have been waiting for this ceremony for 30 years. I can't begin to describe my feelings. This is total freedom," said Saad al-Masoudi, a 40-year-old resident of Karbala, as he walked in a colorful procession. Under Saddam's Sunni-dominated regime, Shiite celebrations were tightly controlled and self-flagellation was banned.

The media also reported on Tuesday insurgents threw a grenade into a Humvee as it drove down a Baghdad street, killing one 1st Armored Division soldier and wounding another.

Joint Contracting Office, Baghdad, 1000 Hours Charlie, Saturday, 06Mar2004

To give you an idea of what we deal with every day, below are samples of the letters we often receive in the Joint Contracting Office from local Iraqi contractors bidding on our requisitions for equipment, supplies, and services:

> dear sir dave conklin
> our company (squaer company) send a prices for barrires concrete no. w91yd6420046 0203. colud you tell us yuor anser pls. and we hope work too geather. cus we work befor that in many baess of usa army like in 2 ACR,,,, RSS. and
> we have Certificate of Appreciation from Regimental command sergeant magor P. BLACKWOOD. (2ACR)...i hope find uoyr anser in e-mail address......
> thank you so much.......

AND:

> Dar Sir:
> With as for pure estimation, we come for your circle the price for the generator is in order of the desired specifications. The generator price ($)

AND:

> Dear Mr. SGT WEATHERLY, TITD.Property NEC.
> 1. I oblogize form you about my late that happend for not answering your E-mail that you send as soon as possible because I was not been able to find a supplier for the bulltproof / seftey glass. Because the amount was to small and no bady can bring it from Jorden or Belgom
> 2. Now WE are ready for supply it in a period less than a week after your agreement on the symbole
> Mr. Awash

AND a note from our Joint Contracting Office Commanding Officer Navy CDR David Sutton:

Not sure what "sttaf" means (see the e-mail below) but never-the-less an encouraging e-mail from one of our contractors. Looks like procedural changes we made are being favorably noticed by contractors.

    To all in the Baghdad Office...this is why we do things the way we do and treat all contractors evenly. We want to be viewed by all our contractors this way. Keep up the ethical and fair dealing with our contractors. This is a positive reflection on all of us.

David

From: "najah jabbar"
To: davespy18@yahoo.com
Subject: thanks for your sttaf
Date: Tue, 09 Mar 2004 14:55:50 +0000
Good evening Miss
We are grateful for contracting offices' sttaf for the way of solicitation awarded.
This way is fair and involve all contracters equally.
For example in the past
1. The tenders lifted from the board before date close.
2. The invitation was special for a few contracters.
3. Some offerers were droped away without you see them.
4. Some offerers were opened in order to know the price.
Now all the items above not found
thank you very much.

AND:

From: Keith T
Date: Sun, 18 Apr 2004 19:33:05 +200400
Allcon,
I'm Having a special on HAV's (Heavy Armored Vehicles) while supplies last.
All vehicles have Level IV B6 Armor protection
Delivery Timeframe: 5 DAYS AFTER CONFIRMATION OF ORDER, FOB Baghdad, Iraq
Models Offered:

10 each 2004 GMC/ Chevrolet Suburbans @ USD $170,000.00 each
2 each 2004 AM General H2 Hummers @ USD $ 187,500.00 each
1 each 2004 BMW X5 @ USD $179,000.00 each
If interested, drop me a line or give me a call
Regards,
Keith T
Country Manager
Saudi Naval Support Company Ltd.
www.snscl.com

AND:

Dear Sir.
reference to the RFQ W913TE-4134-0001, supply of concrete tower.
Would like to inform you that on the IBC web, the original form shows issue date of 25 JUNE and the quote due by date is 24 JUNE, while on the headline shows 25 JUNE.
This tower is pure 100% our design and make, and we are the only manufacturer for it, we have supplied under our company name to KBR-RIO which have been installed in kirkiuk military base, also we supply the private construction companies who win the tenders.
therefore, and due to high security reason and unrest conditions within the coming few days, we prefer to discuss this with you after 1st of june, for a reason that terrorists knows we are the only supplier and they attacked our tracks several times on the way to alaconda and to Tikrit. we will be glad to cooperate with you after 1st JUNE
regards,
captain Sadiq al-hammamy
chairman, shanasheel general construction ltd.

Al Rasheed Hotel, Green Zone, 1920 Hours Charlie, Sunday, 07Mar2004

This evening I decided to change into my PT uniform and get some exercise by running the two miles or so to the Al Rasheed Hotel where I could then eat dinner. Then I would go to the shuttle bus stop between the hotel and the convention center across the street and ride the 7:20 p.m. shuttle bus back. It sounded like a good idea. It was a bad idea.

As soon as I heard the first rocket strike, I said "let's all get off the bus!" There was a rush for the open door as the ten of us hastily ran out and over to the nearby concrete bunker next to the bus stop. I watched just outside the bunker as another and another and another "swoosh, flash, boom!" hit on the other side of the hotel until it seemed like 7 or 8 rockets had struck—but who was counting? It seemed to be over but after about a minute one last boom went off--which I later found out was a car bomb.

The excitement seemed to be over and no one was hurt, but just in case it wasn't over I decided that a moving target would be harder to hit than a stationary one and suggested we should go. But the bus driver, a man in his 60s with a white stubbly beard and a southern drawl refused to come out of the bunker. I decided to hitchhike and if that didn't pan out, to run back the way I came. The first two SUVs that came out of the parking lot sped past without even slowing down, but the third, a black Ford Expedition driven by a lady with a Texas drawl stopped and picked me up.

We sped down the deserted streets and she dropped me outside the finance building near my room. As I walked in, the first floor lobby was full of finance troops who had evacuated the upper floors after the siren at CPA headquarters sounded the alert. The siren is always followed by a loudspeaker announcement "all personnel take cover." We have learned that the attack is always over by the time we hear this announcement. So I went upstairs, took a shower, and turned on the radio. The BBC world news was on, and already had the story. Apparently 10 Russian-made Katyusha rockets were fired from a white Toyota Land Cruiser just outside the Green Zone aimed at the Baghdad Convention Center, a major coalition building where the U.S. military press office is based, and the Al Rasheed Hotel where I just had dinner.

Staff Sergeant Dave Conklin surveys damage to the shuttle bus stop caused by another rocket attack on the Al Rasheed Hotel Sunday Apr 12, 2004. (DCP2177) (Photo --Dave Conklin)

Later, other members of my detachment: Air Force CPT Cathy Blacklock, SSG Craig Durnell, and DOD civilian Lea McDaniel, also came back from the Al Rasheed where they arrived just after I left. Craig said they had just put their food on the table when the first rocket hit. They dropped to the floor when the next one hit, and began low crawling away from the windows. He said, "Every time a rocket hit it lifted me off the floor. I've never been so scared. My stomach felt like I had just come down the big drop on a roller coaster ride." As soon as the attack ended, he said everyone was herded into the basement and kept there for another hour. The most recent nearby rocket attack before this was on the evening of March 3rd, only four days ago, but it was only a single rocket, hardly worth noting.

Bangor, Maine, 1652 Hours Victor, Tuesday, 09Mar2004

My retired Navy submariner friend from Maine writes:

Hi Dave,

It's good to hear from you. Rod and I met last week when he was in Caribou to get his taxes done. We both wondered if you were OK, since we hadn't heard from you for a while. Glad all is well. I think I heard about the rocket attack and the car bomb on the news. Hearing about it from you is a bonus. I trust your journal will develop into a book upon your return.

Rod is getting ready for the bear season. He's overbooked for the first three weeks, and we're going to party the fourth week. COL Sam is going to return this year. We'll miss not having you here.

Rod told me how you went from LTC to SSG. I remember when I was working out of Japan 1965-68 the Army got hold of Navy guys who had a GCT/ARI of 120 or more and offered us Warrant Officer rank to learn how to become helicopter pilots. The bad news, besides being in a real dangerous profession, was getting rifted back to enlisted pay grade when we had the audacity to survive or dropped out for some reason. At least you'll get to retire as O-5. Your time investment is too great to back out now. Keep the stories coming. Stay safe.

Tommy

Then I write to a title company about buying a house while I am still in Iraq:

Ms. Harris, attorney for Southland Title Company:

Thanks for the note. My wife Mary has full Power of Attorney (PoA) for me while I am in Iraq, a copy of which was sent to M&T Mortgage Co. In addition I have also signed before a notary your special power of attorney as requested and e-mailed it to M&T and Southland. In addition I have also sent the original to M&T Mortgage last week because I didn't have a mailing address for Southland.

I tried to Fed Ex the PoA to Southland but the last rocket attack here forced them to close up for a few days. I was going to wait until they opened again but my unit was not going to risk getting a convoy ambushed so I could send a letter. I hate to be grouchy, but communication isn't always easy in a combat zone halfway around

the world from Palm Springs. I hope we can still close the house on schedule and I apologize for the inconvenience.
Sincerely,
David G. Conklin

Green Zone, Baghdad, 2252 Hours Charlie, Monday, 15Mar2004

I write to my youngest sister to answer some questions about how I do my journal:

Lori:
Thanks for the note. I try to write my notes as soon as I can before I forget the details, then tidy them up later to send out. They won't all be in order, but you can arrange them by date. I'm trying to find the time to write while everything is new and before my senses get numbed (see below) by time and routine. By the way, if there is anything the museum wants (Iraqi medals, rank insignia, money, weapons, etc.) and can tell me how to legally send it to them let me know. We got a shitload of AK-47s around here. It seems like every country in the Middle East makes them. More later.
Dave

Wolf Pack Dining Facility, Green Zone, 1845 Hours Charlie, Tuesday, 16Mar2004

I keep in shape not only by wearing 45-pounds of body armor and loaded rifle magazines during the day, but also by working out when I can. Today I was able to get in a twenty-minute run in the supposedly safe Green Zone before dark. I ran through an Iraqi neighborhood (yes Iraqis live here too) as I sometimes do and children would wave and I would wave back and say *marhaba* or hello. Some would be walking behind their veiled mothers, others were on bicycles, one small girl ran a little with me, and another dark-skinned boy about 8 years old even grabbed my arm and tried to get me to stop for a while. "*La, la, la*" (no, no, no) I replied as I wanted to get back before dark. It was good that I did, as I had heard stories of soldiers getting their throats cut at night—even in the Green Zone. In fact CPT Fessenbecker at the 31st Combat Support Hospital just the other day admitted a soldier who was seriously slashed with a knife while walking through the trailer court near the CPA in Saddam's former Presidential Palace.

I returned to our building just in time to get a ride with CPT Blacklock and the others to the evening meal. When I first arrived in Baghdad I really liked the fact that there were three dining facilities and soldiers can eat at any one of them. What a change from Camp Udairi in the Kuwaiti desert. Since I'm working 12 hours a day 6 days a week from 8 to 5 and then again from 8 p.m. to 11 p.m. at night, the highlight of my day is the dinner break. But now a little more than a month later, everyone I went with had a favorite place NOT to eat. CPT Blacklock didn't want to eat at the CPA dining room because of the recent knife attack outside. Air Force SSG Durnell refused to eat at the Al Rasheed Hotel because of last week's rocket attack. SGT Chappell won't eat at the Wolf Pack Dining Hall because of the hassle getting through security (even though I think it has the best food and the two-day laundry is nearby).

The Wolf Pack is run by contractors Kellogg, Brown & Root (KBR) and is the dining facility (DFAC) used by the 2nd Armored Cavalry Regiment (2nd ACR), headquartered nearby. Security at the front gate has always been tight, because it is only a few yards from the busiest and most dangerous entrance to the Green Zone, Checkpoint 2. Since the January car bombing Checkpoint 2 is now known as Assassin's Gate. There are gate guards from the 2nd ACR, tire rippers, a vehicle maze, a machine gun nest, and mandatory stops to clear weapons. We figure that the 2nd ACR also wanted more chow for their own troops because in February they started checking ID cards at the Wolf Pack DFAC. Anytime you forgot yours, you couldn't get in. We figured that was OK if it kept the private mercenaries out, who were mostly Brits anyway.

Entrance to Wolfpack Dining Facility near Assassin's Gate in the Green Zone, Baghdad Wednesday Mar 17, 2004. (DCP02076) (Photo --Dave Conklin)

Then the 2nd ACR went and banned all vehicles without dispatch logs. If you didn't have a log, you had to park near Assassin's Gate and walk a half-mile. Sometimes I even ended my run at the chow hall, but who wanted to do this day after day? Since our non-tactical vehicles were confiscated they weren't dispatched. So to get around that I generated my own dispatch log for each vehicle and signed out one to myself each time. Since this new requirement reduced the line of vehicles waiting to get their IDs and dispatches checked, we figured this would still be OK if it kept the Brits out.

Then the 2nd ACR posted a 10 kph speed limit—that's slower than walking! OK we needed time to get in the mood for a good dinner. But then last week they moved the concrete Jersey rails to block off the entire gravel parking area near the dining facility. Tonight we again walked across the empty parking lot to get in. But the strategy seemed to be working for the 2nd ACR. There were no mercenaries, no Brits, and in fact hardly anyone from outside the 2nd ACR compound that could get in to eat anymore! Just think how much money they are saving the government on food bills! As for me, I brought back a couple of boxes of Frosted Flakes and milk from the chow hall tonight and will be enjoying tomorrow's breakfast at my desk in the office.

> Dear Mary:
> Thanks for our granddaughter's baby shower photos and the bouncing heart! I think a great name for her would be Isabella Guerra! All is well except that I try to do too much as usual. Me and another guy are taking Arabic lessons 3 times a week also. They write from right to left so that's good for a left-hander like me! Here's a photo of me outside the post office near the airport where we went to mail my card to you last Sunday. By the way I met some Spanish troops here but the Spanish people are falling right into the terrorists trap after the recent train bombing in Spain. As usual it looks like CNN is doing a better job with intelligence than our CIA. I just felt a mortar hit outside somewhere. As long as it's not too loud I don't even bother to go check anymore.
> Love, Dave

My former Montana National Guard Broadcast Detachment Commander writes me back:

> From: "Hampa, Lori L CPT"

To: David Conklin
Subject: Reading you loud and clear
Date: Mon, 15 Mar 2004 08:55:07 -0700
LTC,
Wonderful and thank you! I know the MHS will be very happy to get copies of your journal for our archives. As you well understand, as folks come back from the desert they are reluctant to provide copies of their journals as it is still too fresh and personal –in time we may get a copy of one or two if we're lucky; so, your chronological records are jewels. Keep your head down friend, but not too low that you miss things (doubtful!). Keeping the Homefront hearths burning,
L. Hampa-Chamberlin

Mount Lebanon Hotel, Karada District, Baghdad, 2000 Hours Charlie, Wednesday, 17Mar2004

Hi Lori:
    Thanks for the note. Here is my latest news flash:
I felt a WUMP where I'm living at 8 p.m. tonight and later saw from our rooftop that the SOBs blew up the Mt Lebanon Hotel just across the river. Our translator Dr. Moyaad Razzook just missed a bomb in a trash can this afternoon that was set off when a Humvee went by and injured a soldier.
    Four soldiers in my unit were also injured this morning. They were driving on Route Irish to Camp Victory to get the mail in a leased SUV when the driver changed lanes too abruptly, overcorrected and rolled the vehicle, injuring all four of them. They had their helmets on but not their seatbelts. Luckily the worst injury was a compound wrist fracture and lots of bruises. Another unit totaled a leased Chevy Suburban when the driver tried to pass a water truck on the right at high speed and ran into a concrete barrier. There may not be many laws here, but the "law of gross tonnage" has severe penalties when violated. It gets a little more interesting every day. I'll keep you posted.
Dave C

Mitsubishi Pajero damage from rollover that injured 4 soldiers on the Matar Saddam al-Dowli Expressway (better known as Route Irish), Baghdad Wednesday Mar 17, 2004.
(DCP02080) (Photo --Dave Conklin)

Green Zone, Baghdad, 2000 Hours Charlie, Thursday, 18Mar2004
Hi Lori:

Thanks for the news update and good wishes. The terrorists are stepping up attacks to put an exclamation point on their success in blowing up a train back in Spain. Tonight again, just before 8 p.m., I heard two more explosions here in the Green Zone. By the time I go outside it's usually over and all I hear is the siren and loudspeaker at the CPA telling me to take cover. I can smell the sulphur in the gunpowder if the wind is right. Still safe in Baghdad --Dave C

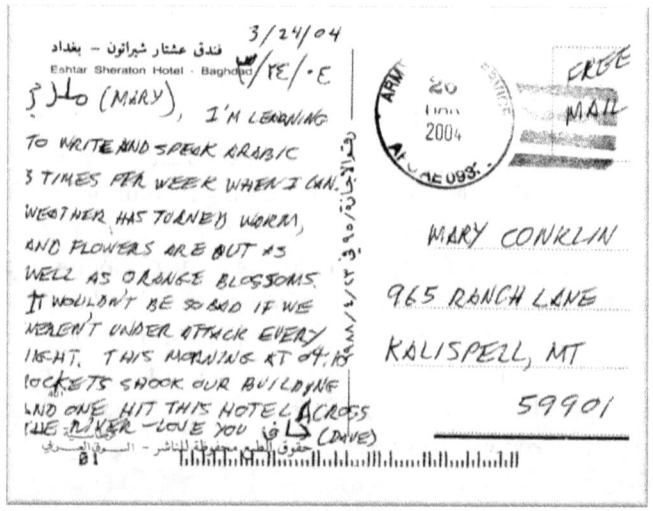

I send another postcard home, this time partially in Arabic
Wednesday, March 24, 2004. (Photo --Dave Conklin)

31st CASH, Baghdad, 1930 Hours Charlie, Monday, 22Mar2004

Today I received a newsy e-mail from a buddy back home and thanked him. It's great hearing about what's going on at home. It helps bring me back to what "reality" should be. Instead, my "typical" Monday in Baghdad went something like this today: When I woke up instead of birds I heard the generator outside my room and a medevac helicopter setting down at the 31st Combat Support Hospital or "CASH" just north of my building. I pulled on my DCUs, grabbed my M16 rifle and headed to the Wolfpack chow hall down the street near the Assassin's Gate for breakfast. Then back for a short lesson to learn Arabic, *Insha Allah* (God willing), followed by a walk to my 350th Civil Affairs Command TOC (Tactical Operations Center) to download financial status data for our civil affairs reconstruction projects.

About 11 a.m. I walked over to the CPA headquarters to pick up a fuel authorization request from the C4 (logistics staff) for our 5 civilian vehicles so we can continue to get fuel at the CPA fuel point. I had lunch in the CPA dining room with our C9 cell operations sergeant MSG Dees to get an update on unit activities. An Apache helicopter circled overhead while I walked back to the Contracting building. There was an Iraqi businessman and woman waiting for me when I returned. They had questions about the latest purchase request I had posted, including "What means post-it note?" Yesterday I asked Nibras, our translator, to call three other successful local bidders and they all came in to sign contracts today. I explained to each one what was expected, when and where to deliver the goods and how to get paid. I needed our interpreter for one bidder, but the other two understood English well enough.

A UH-60 Blackhawk medical evacuation (MEDEVAC) helicopter makes a final approach over the Joint Contracting Building to deliver a patient to the 31st Combat Support Hospital, Green Zone, Baghdad Monday Apr 5, 2004. (DSC00053) (Photo -- Chris Chapple)

The next task was to get our two Toyota Land Cruisers out and check our radios, weapons, and body armor for the trip to Camp Victory to get the mail and deliver some strobe lights purchased for the III Corps C4 by Captain Neel. When we got to the Camp we heard that an IED (Improvised Explosive Device) had injured a soldier on the highway near here today. On the drive back the traffic was light and we arrived at Checkpoint 4 in the Green Zone just before dark without incident. After unloading the mail I went down the street again to eat dinner. On the way back I stopped at the CSH to visit SSG Craig Durnell, our systems technician who was admitted this morning to clear up an infected cut.

In the bed next to him was the soldier who was hit by the IED on the highway today. His co-driver was there and said that the bomb was hidden in a tire alongside the road just before the Camp Victory Checkpoint. The driver's head and leg were bandaged and he was awake but tired after surgery. One piece of shrapnel had torn through his cheek and another had broken all the bones in his lower left leg. The doctor came in and held up a pair of x-rays explaining to him that the bones were now lined up so they would heal, but he could not remove all the pieces of metal. The doc said they would fly him out on the midnight medevac flight to the military hospital in Landstuhl, Germany. I said goodbye to our sergeant and wished the soldier well before making the short walk back to my room for the night. It was a typical end to a typical day here in Baghdad. The sky was a beautiful royal blue and a bright star glowed high above a thin sliver of orange moon just above the western horizon.

Spring flowers bloom along Haifa Street near the Assassin's Gate in Baghdad's Green Zone as soldiers walk from lunch at the Wolf Pack dining hall. Tuesday Mar 23, 2004. (DCP02102) (Photo -- Dave Conklin)

Roof of Contracting and Finance Building, Green Zone, Baghdad, 2030 Hours Charlie, Friday, 26Mar2004

Tonight I got a lesson on smoking the water pipe or "hookah pipe" from our Iraqi linguist Dr. Moyaad Razzook. He has been here since last May. In the Middle East smoking the water pipe and drinking tea is a daily activity where male friends get together and "chew the fat." Besides the pipe, hose, and mouthpiece all you need is a small package of charcoal and flavored tobacco. Not the dry stuff but a bag of semi-damp tobacco, preferably raspberry or strawberry flavored. My favorite is strawberry.

First Moyaad put water in the vase, put the top on, and then put several pieces of charcoal on an electric hot plate. Then he put foil in the perforated ceramic bowl on top and added the tobacco. Next he covered that with foil and punched holes in it for ventilation. Around the ceramic bowl is a metal tray to catch the charcoal as it burns out. Now that the charcoal was hot he broke it into smaller pieces and put them on top of the perforated foil. Then all he had to do was take several deep breaths on the mouthpiece, drawing the hot air from the charcoal down across the tobacco, into the pipe that sticks into the water, then drawing the smoke in the vase above the water into the hose. "Take a deep breath, and then slowly blow the smoke out your nose or mouth," Moyaad said. I found the result is a much milder, sweeter taste than a cigarette and less nicotine and tar. But it still dries out your throat and that is why you want to be drinking tea too. Unfortunately, I also hear that those who smoke the hookah pipe daily will end up with everything from canker sores to lung cancer.

In America these pipes are known as "drug paraphernalia" and customs will not permit us to bring them into the U.S. That is how I got my pipe. SSG Sullivan passed his on to me when he redeployed. Besides, Americans don't have the patience for hookah pipes. If you can't light it with your Zippo and smoke it in three minutes or less, it's not worth the trouble.

60   An Iraq War Diary

Soldiers from the 82nd Airborne Division sample Iraqi water pipes at a vendor in the Al Rasheed Hotel, Green Zone, Baghdad. Sep 10, 2003. (Rasheed Vendor) (Photo -- Sean Sullivan)

Joint Contracting and Finance Office, Baghdad, 0815 Hours Charlie, Saturday, 27Mar2004

"Sabah al Khair!" (good morning) says Dr. Moyaad as he walks through the office. The Iraqi contractors here commonly call him Dr. Moyaad as first names are always used instead of family names when addressing people in Iraq. Moyaad was an Iraqi refugee living in Houston, Texas, who owned a fitness gym with his wife and two daughters when he was recruited by Titan to help interpret for the Americans. After a month of training in Fairfax, Virginia, he came back to Iraq and was the guy who would interpret for the officers who were rounding up and detaining Iraqi troops and terrorists. He quickly got tired of that type of work and asked to be transferred. That's how we found out about him and

got him the job here translating conversations, interpreting letters, and doing background checks on our vendors.

From left: Dr. Moyaad Razzook poses with SSG Dave Conklin, LCDR Kristen Acqavella and the Joint Contracting and Finance Office staff in Baghdad. Tuesday, Apr 21, 2004. (Photo --Dave Conklin)

Moyaad has an interesting past. He is a third generation Baghdadi. He was born on October 27, 1948 and started bodybuilding when he was eleven years old. He graduated from Baghdad University in sports nutrition, during which time he became "Mr. Iraq" in bodybuilding contests. He even competed against Arnold Schwarzenegger in London in 1970. He earned a "full ride" scholarship to do advanced studies at Moscow University in Russia, with a $50 a month stipend. This was a fortune in those days and being a "rich" 22-year-old bodybuilder allowed him to make a lot of friends—of the female kind. Soon the USSR's Secret Service, the KGB, took an interest in him for having so much fun. Then the University extended their PhD Degree Program from five to seven years.

After one year he returned to Baghdad and was lucky enough to get the Ministry of Education to agree to sponsor him again if he could get admitted to a university in the U.S. He did—the University of Florida in Gainesville. After graduation he came back to teach at Baghdad University as he had promised. As is the Arab custom, he grew up in a large extended family, the youngest of four boys, and now married the youngest daughter of his uncle—his first cousin. His older brother, now a dentist in London, of course married her sister, the older daughter of his mother's sister.

So it happened that in 1981 during Saddam's Iran-Iraq war, Moyaad, his wife and daughter were driving near Tikrit when an Iranian jet strafed their car and it rolled over, pinning their daughter underneath. Luck again intervened and when some soldiers helped them turn the car over, they found her in a depression underneath, cut and bruised, but still alive. To this day his sister and family still lives in Baghdad, but Moyaad decided to leave Iraq. He was able to go to Greece and apply for asylum in the U.S. as a war refugee. Being a Catholic Christian, the church sponsored him and paid for his trip to Houston, Texas, where he became a U.S. citizen. During the intervening years he started a Lutheran school in Houston and a bodybuilding gym that he was still operating with a partner until he volunteered to come back to Iraq and help take his country back.

SSG Dave Conklin gets his Arabic language homework from Melad Al Jaburi, one of the Command's interpreter/ translators. Friday, Apr 3, 2004. (DCP02145) (Photo --Dave Conklin)

5. The Coming Storm

Sadr City, Baghdad, 1900 Hours Charlie +1, Sunday, 04Apr2004

The Blackhawks were landing at the combat support hospital in a steady stream now it seemed, dropping their medevac patients and taking off again, the pilots not waiting to retrieve the empty stretchers like they usually do. Something big was going down. Today the Shiite revolt that had been fomenting for weeks erupted into violence and American soldiers were again paying a high price for Iraqi freedom.

I could feel the tension growing for a week or more, ever since the coalition closed down the Al Hawsa newspaper of radical young Shiite cleric Moqtada Al Sadr. I watched the demonstrations last Wednesday afternoon outside the Al Rasheed gate here. Then on the same day four U.S. contractors were killed in an ambush in Fallujah, 35 miles west of here. A crowd of cheering Iraqis dragged their charred and mutilated corpses down the street and hanged them from a bridge over the Euphrates River.

An Iraqi boy flashes the victory sign near a charred body hanging from a bridge over the Euphrates River in the flashpoint town of Fallujah. Angry residents armed with shovels mutilated the charred bodies of two people, believed to be foreigners, caught in an insurgent attack and warned the rebel Iraqi town would be the "cemetery" of U.S. occupation forces. (body)(Photo --AFP/ Sabah Arar)

Saturday we convoyed in our Toyota Land Cruisers to take Air Force SSG Craig Durnell to the airport to catch a C-130 back to his home at Barksdale Air Force Base, Louisiana. His 90-day tour was over but mine had 290 days to go and seemed like it was just beginning. The return trip went fine, up until we reached the Green Zone. An armored personnel carrier blocked Checkpoint 12 due to bomb threats. Now we had to decide how to find our way through the streets of Baghdad to another checkpoint and hope it would be open. I figured moving targets are better than sitting ducks. I noticed the MP convoy of Humvees and 5-ton trucks that we passed earlier was heading north so we followed along sandwiched between two 5-tons in the convoy. We drove north passing stores and open food markets, then east through traffic, past a broken-down bus left in the street, and finally south until we reached Checkpoint 2 which was open by then.

By Sunday morning, all checkpoints in and out of the Green Zone were closed. Apparently Shiite cleric Moqtada Al Sadr announced from his headquarters, a mosque in the city of Kufah south of here, that he was opening Iraqi chapters of Hezbollah and Hamas and urged his militia to "terrorize your enemy." Soon thousands of his private militia, the "Mahdi Army" wearing green headbands and carrying AK-47s and RPGs were taking control of the Sadr City slum in east Baghdad where today's battle raged until dark. Despite reinforcements with tanks and Bradley Armored Fighting Vehicles, eight of our soldiers from the 1st Armored Division were killed and dozens were wounded in the firefight to retake the area. Now the Marines have cordoned off Fallujah and a warrant has been issued for Al Sadr's arrest in Kufah. I'm afraid we'll be seeing more medevac helicopters again soon.

Al Rasheed Hotel, Baghdad, 1430 Hours Charlie +1, Thursday, 08Apr2004

The Al Rasheed Hotel gate guard's uniform had a Totem patch indicating he was with the newly arrived 81st Infantry, Washington National Guard. He said, "You can't park in the parking lot. You have to park on the street, and stay to the right as you walk in." I should have taken the hint and turned around. But I offered to drive SFC Chris Chapple and MSG Arnette Robinson to chow today and they were hungry. Only after we went inside and were not allowed back out were we told that a sharp-eyed contractor had spotted an Improvised Explosive Device, or IED, with a cell phone triggering device under his vehicle in the parking lot. Finally we were allowed to go out the convention center gate and we walked back to our office. We were about a half-mile away when we heard the BANG as the EOD team exploded it in place. Another tactic is to take a grenade and tie it to the undercarriage of a vehicle. Then tie one end of a wire to the pin and the other to a spoke in the wheel rim. As you drive off the pin is pulled. Our response is to always check under our vehicles before we start or move them.

Right: Iraqis loot and burn vehicles after a fatal ambush on a highway on the edge of Baghdad. Gunmen fired on a convoy of sport utility vehicles killing at least two people, one of them an Iraqi bystander and injuring a pregnant woman, witnesses and officials said. Some witnesses and police said that after the SUVs crashed in the hail of bullets, attackers emerged from the oncoming traffic and dragged five or six 'Western-looking men' away. Sunday, May 30, 2004. (Iraq atks)(Photo -- AP)

    Since offensive operations began in Baghdad and Fallujah last Sunday, combat casualties are up to 20 --more than any time since Baghdad fell on April 9th a year ago. A First Lieutenant with the 1st Armored Division came in on Wednesday wearing DCUs with no tags or patches. He said his uniform was burned up in a Humvee crash near Najaf. He also said Al Sadr's followers had staged a "peaceful" demonstration there at the front gates of the Garrison then pushed their way inside knowing we can only shoot them for "hostile acts" under our rules of engagement. Once inside they pulled out AK-47s from under their robes and began shooting. The Ukrainians abandoned the garrison leaving weapons and ammo behind. A captain from FOB Dragoon near Sadr City in east Baghdad said his snipers killed three infiltrators last night within 300 feet of the wire.

    The 2nd ACR was supposed to finally begin redeploying back to Fort Polk this week but was instead pulled out to reinforce other units. CPT Jackson with their regimental support squadron at FOB Muleskinner here in Baghdad came in today to get more money and supplies for his unit.

The sun sets over central Baghdad amid the sounds of helicopters, sporadic automatic weapons fire, and the occasional "ther-WUMP" of mortars landing in the distance. Friday Aug 28, 2004. (P8280014) (Photo --Dave Conklin)

He said their one-year deployment had just been extended another 120 days. Jackson said on a good day it takes about 20 minutes to travel between Muleskinner and the Green Zone but today they spotted 5 IEDs along the road and had to detour and defuse them.

Folks around here are definitely not in a festive mood for the coming Easter weekend. Our Iraqi interpreter Nibras said as she left early today, "I think Saturday and Easter Sunday will be bad days." As for me, after dinner I climbed the stairs to the roof of our building and sat there in a white plastic chair looking at the stars and listening to invisible helicopters, sporadic automatic weapons fire, and the occasional "ther-WUMP" of mortars landing in the distance. From the "sound" of things, I would have to agree with Nibras.

Green Zone, Baghdad, 1100 Hours Charlie +1, Good Friday, 09Apr2004

Friday (in Arabic *al-Jum'a*) began as a clear, warm spring day. All is quiet in the Green Zone as many units have left to reinforce other units now that the Sunni guerillas are on the rampage to the west in Fallujah and the Shiite guerillas to the south in Najaf. But guerillas have become bolder even in Baghdad during the last few days. As I look to the west I can see a cloud of black smoke from a tanker truck destroyed by gunmen this morning on the main highway to the airport, the same road we have to use tomorrow and again on Monday to get three of our soldiers and a civilian on a C-130 back to the states.

Our team gets ready to convoy to the airport and to Camp Victory for the mail. Back from left to right: SSG JJ Orr, SFC Chris Chapple, CDR Dave Sutton, SSG Craig Durnell; front: SSG Dave Conklin, Saturday Apr 3, 2004. (DSC07983) (Photo --Dave Conklin)

One of my former Army commanders back home writes:

> David, how come the other guys in the photo have guns and you only have a camera? Watch yourself. --Chuck

We are worried that things could quickly spin out of control if both tribal factions convince other Iraqis that Coalition forces are attacking Iraqis indiscriminately. Others tell me that only brute force will put down Al

Sadr's militia and the Sunnis in Fallujah, just as Saddam controlled Al Sadr's father and uncle by killing them.

Coalition operations will also be hampered by hundreds of thousands of pilgrims going to southern cities, particularly Karbala, to attend al-Arbaeen ceremonies this weekend to mark the end of the period of mourning for a 7th-century martyred Shiite saint. Guerillas have now taken Japanese, Korean, and even Arab hostages, threatening to burn the three Japanese alive unless troops are removed. Any light-skinned person is now in danger on the streets of Baghdad.

Another friend writes:
> Sad to say...but the North Vietnamese did the same thing... It was called "Tet"...and one of the most Holy days of the year, with fireworks, displays, thousands of religious visitors going throughout the country side, Saigon streets jammed, etc. And then they launch a massive attack throughout the country. "Hunker down" David . . . we're praying for you. --JLM

Al-Firdaws District, Baghdad, 1118 Hours Charlie +1, Saturday, 10Apr2004

Meeting an M1 Abrams Main Battle Tank head-on at a combined speed of 150km per hour was not the way I pictured myself going out of this world, but there it was coming directly at us on "our" side of the expressway. Luckily we saw it just in time to squeeze into the only lane that the tank didn't occupy. In rapid succession we went past a burned out Hyundai SUV in the median, an eighteen-wheeler that was still on fire on the opposite on-ramp, a fallen lamppost in the center lane, and guardrails blown out by IEDs before reaching the checkpoint to the airport. After dropping off Navy CDR Sutton so he could fly home to his family after 6 months in Iraq we were informed that about 50 others didn't make his flight because the bus was cancelled due to a gunfight earlier this morning at the checkpoint we just came through.

A burning big rig blocks an on-ramp to the Matar Saddam Al-Dowli Expressway after guerilla attacks on Saturday Apr 10, 2004. (DCP2166) (Photo --Dave Conklin)

As we walked into the Bob Hope Dining Facility near the airport for lunch, we heard a couple of mortar rounds impact in the distance. After I picked up the mail, we locked and loaded our weapons for the return trip. The highway was pretty much deserted during our mid-afternoon drive back, except for the wreckage from the attacks this morning. As we drove past Checkpoint 12 into the Green Zone we heard mortars impacting somewhere ahead of us, and by the time we reached our building a fire truck was following behind to put out the resulting fire. It turns out the mortars hit just a block from our building. Later this evening MSG Robinson who stayed behind said of our other driver, "I think today got to him. This is the first time I've seen the sergeant really worried enough to not be able to focus on his work." I think maybe it's because he knows that we have to go again on Monday.

Baghdad, Iraq, 0800 Hours Charlie +1, Easter Sunday, 11Apr2004
    To all My Friends and Family:
Happy Easter to all and thanks for your letters and care packages. The Arabic word for resurrection is *Ba'ath*. We can all hope for our own and this country's resurrection someday. It's too bad that Saddam Hussein used the same word for his political party, but this is only one of the many things that are hard to understand in the Middle East.
Have a great Easter.
Dave C

My cousin Susie writes back:

> It's Easter Sunday......I was having coffee watching the sun rise with the peacocks, when along came a coyote to disrupt the peace and contemplation. . . I pray to god--or whatever spiritual energy there

may be--that you guys make it through this day in one piece. You may have heard this before (I know--Mrs. Zurich!), but my Dad was in the Navy for 11 years and would have been a lifer if not for his wife Dottie. He was part of the occupation forces in Japan after the war. This changed him forever. My Mom says he was a different person when he came back. Once he had drive and optimism, but was considered "lazy" and pessimistic when back in civilian life (I know your dad felt this way about him. He told me so during a heated discussion after Joanie died). Smiley never talked about the war . . . never wanted to discuss battles etc. I do know he saw his best friend get his head blown off. I know how upset he was to see the civilians in Japan living like animals in the streets after the H-bomb. I know he was opposed to the Vietnam War and would have sent Steve to Canada had he been drafted. I guess what I'm trying to say is I know you have the compassion my Dad did . . . you truly feel for the people. I just hope your "military indoctrination" doesn't blind you of reality. Take care, David. Please keep in touch.–Susie S.

Susie:
Thanks for the words. That explains a lot. Remember, it's not what happens to you, or around you . . . but how you deal with it that counts.
Dave

I received this from a Marine Corps Chaplain in Fallujah:

It is Hot and sunny on Good Friday . . . quiet in Fallujah and Ar Ramadi. The Coalition has announced a pause in offensive operations. Humanitarian Aid is being searched and then allowed into the city of Fallujah. Defensive operations continue 24/7. It is all war, all the time. The bad guys are regrouping. So are the Marines. The brawl will begin again...probably tonight. All intel points to the bad guys redistributing ammo, enlisting kids in the fight and moving for new cover. Convoys are limited . . . danger of ambush is high.

Life in Blue Diamond continues, with an edge. Imagine a place the size of Lakeland Shores (Minnesota) with 5 times the population. One asphalt street, two dirt roads. Due to the siege no sanitation service for three days, that includes pumping satellites. We are on the edge of the town. We see the minarets of the city and we hear the imams' sermons as they rail against us. Good thing few here understand Arabic cause I can tell you the preachers weren't teaching the golden rule today.

Morale sky high, extra intensity, friends are on the line. The senior NCO's and officers here feel the pull the most. They have served with or trained everyone on the line. The Marine Corps is a small community. This is very personal. If a person can do something to help the outcome of the fight they'll find a way. It's that kind of day--all for one, one for all.

I divide the day; Holy Week service planning, convoy prayers, and COC (Command Operations Center) intercessory prayer.

First--I go to the DIV Chaplains office to meet with the command Chaplain, Chaplain Divine, the fighting Irishman. What a man. RC Christians be proud you've got a great priest here. He spares nothing to get to his marines. He loves marines and he loves God. He waded into Ar Ramadi during the firefight three days ago to provide ministry at the aid station, came back weary but satisfied he was where he was needed. He's on the road to all the FOBs ministering to marines. I had the privilege of praying for him this morning. If he goes down the morale in this Division would take a huge hit. They love him.

Second--I work to coordinate Good Friday, Easter Sunrise and Protestant Easter Service. Having services in a war zone is a little different.

A) We have to worry about getting large numbers of people in one place. One mortar round into the right place and you could kill a lot of marines.

B) Organists are in short supply and we don't have an organ. Music?

C) We are going to worship and it will be well attended. We need Easter because we live in the valley of the shadow of death. We need the resurrection.

Third--Twice a day I go to the 'Cave' (Combat Operations Center) that is housed in a former palace poorly lit and the hub of fighting the battle. I stand in the corner and pray for each person/ position and those they represent. I don't know many of them, but God does. I pray for wisdom, strength, mercy, endurance and God's presence for each warrior all those they serve or represent. I cover the Cave and the battlefield as I look at live imagery projected on the wall. I don't know how the marines do it but the COC is loaded with stark looking marines. The senior NCO's all look like NFL linemen. The junior officers look like marathon runners and the mid-grade officers look like NFL halfbacks. The senior officers are lean, tanned and serious --deadly serious. The place exudes the warrior spirit. If you are a civilian I can't explain it and won't apologize for it. If you are a veteran you don't need me to explain the warrior spirit.

These Marines are in a street fight. They don't have the word 'lose' in their vocabulary. They've been bloodied and their anger is up. The intensity in the COC is contagious. This is a tribe of warriors. They exist to close with and destroy the enemy. They have their tribal mores, rituals and rites. Their enemy has desecrated members of the tribe and taunted the marines. They've asked for a fight. The marines are in full pursuit and absolutely determined to annihilate their foe. I'm sure that sounds harsh to politically correct ears and those for whom this type of violence is anachronistic. It does not sound foreign here. It is status quo. We are in a violent land with an evil element and they are having violence visited upon them. There is no room here for half measures. This is a test of wills. One side will prevail. That is clearly understood and never discussed. It is obvious. We aren't playing paintball. We are at war.

Fourth--Convoy prayers. Convoys go out of here regularly. I hunt them down, pass out a small card with a convoy prayer on it and then gather whoever wants to pray and we pray. The number of prayers is going up, hourly, as the ambushes continue. Here's how intense it has become. Today's standard pre-convoy brief now includes the following: "If you drive into the kill zone--two options: 1) drive through and on, or 2) reverse and drive out. Do not stop. If you are blocked into the kill zone displace from the vehicle, find cover, fix the target, engage, maneuver and destroy the hostile forces. Target selection rules have changed. Avoid civilians if possible. Hostile forces are now using civilians as shields. We are not interested in losing more Marines. If you can avoid putting civilians in your line of fire avoid it. If not, fire to take out the hostile forces. Implication?

Chilling, we've entered a new dimension. We are fighting an enemy who respects no laws of humanity, knows no rules of land warfare and gives no quarter. How do we fight without becoming barbarians ourselves?

Fifth--Ministry of presence. In a place this small I walk from shop to shop and just say, "Hi" and I can't tell you the number of times someone says, "Hey chappy it's great to have you here." Something about seeing a chaplain is calming to folks this close to the fight. Good Friday in Ar Ramadi. While you're having lunch I'll lead the evening Good Friday service. We will remember our Savior who willingly laid down His life that we might live and we'll be thinking about young Marines and soldiers who willingly put their lives on the line so Iraqis can be free. No greater love hath a man than to lay down his life for his brother. Good Friday to you. --John

Green Zone, Baghdad, 0420 Hours Charlie +1, Monday, 12Apr2004

Easter Sunday was quiet for the most part, but Monday began with a bang—literally! The first one woke me at 4:20 a.m. It turned out to be an RPG round that blew up the bus stop at the Al Rasheed Hotel about a mile from our building. This was the day we were scheduled to take three of our folks to the airport for their departure from Iraq, and they were anxious to go! The vehicles were loaded by 8 a.m. and I had just put on my body armor and Kevlar helmet and was outside when the rocket hit. Woosh—KaBAM! It gouged a hole in the street about 50 meters from our wall in a big puff of smoke. GET DOWN I yelled to Dr. Moyaad Razzook our translator who was standing next to the Toyota with me. As we dropped we could hear pieces of metal falling out of the sky like steel rain all around us, making clinking sounds as they bounced off the pavement. Luckily no one was hit. Miraculously the falling shrapnel even missed the car that I just replaced the windshield on from a similar incident. As others came outside to see what was happening I yelled to them to get back inside and closed the door behind us as we ran inside the building.

When I didn't hear any more bangs, I decided it was time for us to get out of there. The traffic was light on the way to the airport due to recent ambushes and snipers. It was a lot like driving in Washington D.C. after a sniper attack. By the way, the taxi drivers don't speak English here either! We passed a fuel truck convoy that had traffic backed up behind it.

SSG Dave Conklin inspects a smoldering piece of the rocket that hit the wall of the Contracting Office parking lot after blowing up in the street near the north gate of the CPA Presidential Palace in the Green Zone on Monday Apr 12, 2004. (DCP2170) (Photo --Dave Conklin)

At the airport we delivered our soldiers to the passenger terminal tent as three mortars landed somewhere near the runway. I asked one young soldier if he was flying home. No such luck. He said he was trying to get a flight back to his unit in Mosul after his convoy was shot up in an ambush. His unit didn't know where he was yet, maybe even a hostage as far as they knew. He said there was a fuel truck burning next to the road that had been hit earlier. Then when his convoy went by, the insurgents detonated a bomb at the truck that spread the smoke and flames. As soon as they drove out of the smoke they were targeted by small arms and RPGs. He said they returned fire and killed at least two, but one female truck driver was hit in the neck and another female truck driver was "freaking out." They had to abandon some trucks and turn around and head back to Baghdad with what they had left and get the wounded soldier to the hospital.

We were ready to go back now, but I received a phone call from our office and we had to wait at the airport because Checkpoint 12 was closed until an IED could be defused, and we found out that our new commander, Navy LCDR Kristen Acqavella, a Supply Corps Officer from NAVSEA at the Washington D.C. Navy Yard would arrive today. Also another contracting replacement Air Force TSgt Mike Birkland, a native Montanan now based at Elmendorf Air Force Base in Anchorage, Alaska had flown in and we needed to bring them both back. The C-130 landed on time and we found them by the nametags on their uniforms. We were anxious to get back after being in full "battle rattle" all day so we gave them a quick safety brief, put their bags in our Toyotas, locked and loaded our weapons and headed out with them in the back seat.

Apparently I had already forgotten how much of a culture shock it is to arrive in a combat zone until one of them asked, "Do we put the bullets in our pistols now?" To which I replied, "That's why they gave you the gun isn't it?" A little later, after listening to mortar strikes, passing burned out trucks and dusty convoys of tanks and Bradleys I turned around to see one of them losing their lunch in the back seat. At the end of the trip I'm sure they were as happy to get inside our building as I was when I first got here.

Green Zone, Baghdad, 2200 Hours Charlie +1, Thursday, 15Apr2004
My sister writes:
Wow, looks like things are getting worse. Are we getting more help for your guys over there?? The Shiites are bad Muslims yes? Your HASH Iraqi's are the good guys yes? Stay safe, does not look like it's getting better. Xoxoxo SOOOOOOOOOOOOOO Happy to see your e-mail. --- xoxoxo Rita

Hi Rita:
Thanks for writing. Check out my latest messages for the latest SITREP. So far I am fine (just heard another mortar hit outside as I am writing this).
Love you. --Dave.

What is SITREP???   --XO Rita

Rita:
Thanks for writing. In answer to your questions, A SITREP is Army lingo for a "situation report." The Brits are to the south in Basra. The other coalition forces are holed up in their camps. We are putting together about two or three-thousand soldiers to go after the bad guys. --Dave

Camp Steel Falcon, Green Zone, 0830 Hours Charlie +1, Saturday, 17Apr2004
When the guys came back from chow this morning they said, "Don't bother going to lunch today. The dining facility is running short of food and is only serving breakfast and dinner because the convoys are being ambushed." In fact only yesterday I heard BG Mark Kimmitt, Assistant

Chief of Operations, say at his daily briefing that the main supply routes, or MSRs to the south, west and north of Baghdad are still under attack and the supply situation would get worse before it got better. So MREs will be our only option for lunch other than what we can have our Iraqi workers buy for us in Baghdad.

SSG Dave Conklin is the Humvee turret gunner during a Civil Affairs mission in Baghdad on a hot Tuesday Aug 25, 2004. (P8250150) (Photo -- Dave Conklin)

Today five more Marines died in an ambush in Husaybah on the Syrian border. The ambush, started by hundreds of rebel gunners, helped make April the deadliest month since the war in Iraq began, with 100 American soldiers killed so far. We are hearing rumors now that the Spanish and Hondurans are pulling their troops out entirely which may cause the rebels to be even bolder.

Raheem Waddah, one of my Iraqi contractors, a tall honest-looking man with black hair and a dark complexion, came in for a payment and apologized for not coming in for the past two weeks. Bandits killed his younger brother last week while he was delivering a generator to the Americans. He was 36 years old. Raheem said it was dangerous for Iraqis to come to the American camps now. He said he has been able to do well in business since Saddam was removed, but now the rebels threaten everyone that helps the Americans. "Everyone must carry a gun to protect himself," he said. "They have even taken Iraqi businessmen hostage and threaten to cut off their heads unless their families pay a ransom so the rebels can buy more weapons. Criminals and thieves have even become a big problem because there are so few policemen," Raheem said.

Checkpoint 12, Green Zone, Baghdad, 1530 Hours Charlie +1, Tuesday, 20Apr2004

I was surprised as we braked to a stop at Checkpoint 12. For the first time we were the only vehicles entering. There always seemed to be a line-up here, but not today. Even the traffic was light both going out of Baghdad and coming back. There were no delays today outside of some slower Humvee and Hemmet truck convoys, a few Bradleys and tanks traveling down the expressway in the proper direction for a change, and an occasional broken guardrail in the fast lane. But none of the burned out trucks and vans from last week's attacks had been cleaned up either.

A 1st Cavalry Division soldier mans his M249 Squad Automatic Weapon (SAW) from the comfort of a car seat mounted on the back of his disabled Humvee as it is towed down the highway west of Baghdad Tuesday Apr 20, 2004. (DCP2202) (Photo --Dave Conklin)

Our weekly mail run was delayed a day this week because our new commander called the Force Protection office yesterday at the CPA and asked for the road condition report. They said it was "amber." She then asked, "If you were us, would you go?" and they replied "No." So she cancelled the trip. Later she asked how often the road condition was "amber" and SFC Chapple said "it's always amber except for when it's red—but that means it's closed." Since the Air Force and Navy folks deploy with only 9mm pistols, which are worthless in an ambush, I passed out the AK-47s and MP-5s that we had on hand and showed them how to load them. I'm not sure the lesson took as this supply corps officer tried to push the MP-5 magazine into the hole in the pistol grip. "The main thing," I said, "is to keep the safety on and don't point it at me."

But my "lesson learned" for today would have to be that my cousin Susie was right—I'm not normal! This revelation came to me after we returned today and I mentioned how nice it was to get out in the sunshine and go for a drive at least once a week. Just about everyone else said they were petrified by this and every trip we make "outside the wire" in camouflage uniforms, in vehicles bristling with loaded rifles, 2-way radios, first aid kits and emergency rations. That's when I realized that while they had never done this before, to me it was no big deal. Why? Because I have done it many times before. In fact in Montana every fall I go for a drive in vehicles bristling with loaded rifles, 2-way radios, first aid kits and emergency rations to try to kill things—we call it "hunting season." The big difference of course is that deer don't shoot back!

> Dave,
> Got a great kick out of the Navy Commander trying to load the MP-5. I learned the hard way with that piece of just where the gas port was located in relation to the sight pictured during sustained fire. Right into the right eyeball! I loved that thing with the suppressor. Yes, being a hunter contributes to survival experience. And that can make all the difference.
> Stay safe, Tommy

Green Zone, Baghdad, 2315 Hours Charlie +1, Wednesday, 21Apr2004
Dear Mary:
Yes and No to your last e-mail question and picture. Yes the camel spider exists but no it will not harm you and it's only about the size of the palm of your hand (amazing what camera lenses can do!). I have had this same picture with the same question sent to me by 3 different people now, including catalog sales departments. When I find one I'll take its picture and send you a full report.

Supply lines must be improving a little--got a lettuce salad for dinner for the first time in 2 weeks. Hooray! (Have to look for reasons to be happy you know). A mortar attack at the Camp yesterday killed 22 Iraqi prisoners and injured 92. It's near the passenger terminal at the airport where we were a week ago Monday. I'll send you another story tonight if I have time.
Love you much.
Dave

Bozeman, Montana, 0921 Hours Tango +1, Thursday, 22Apr2004
My daughter writes:
   Hey Dad:
   I talked with Justin's teacher, Barb Pierre, and she said that they would be happy to "sponsor a soldier" so to speak. (That's what I called it anyway) They will be drawing pictures and stuff and I will send them to you in a care package every so often. She was wondering if you could also e-mail the class and send pictures. I thought that would be a great idea. This gives the kids a face behind the conflict and not just what is happening in the news. So let me know what you need from time to time and I will send a care package off with the help of Mrs. Pierre's fourth grade class. Maybe you could send something really cool from the Middle East that the class could learn from. Maybe some money if you still have some, that would be awesome!!
   I plan on going to Kalispell next weekend to pay bills and stuff. Mom says it has been really slow. That will help her out with the cleaning and de-winterizing the house and grounds. I talk to her every day so she won't miss me. In fact she is probably sick of me interrupting her every day with a "what's up" phone call. I think with Rachelle moving in with her in May will be great for her. Not just monetarily, but also for the company.
   Today it is supposed to be 68 degrees. The sun is shining and it is a beautiful day. I am just waiting for a phone call from Chris to let me know when his baby is coming. Today is the due date. Hopefully she will be on time. Justin is missing you and hopes you will come back "in one piece." I am working on an end-of-season write up for CSI Tours. I am waiting on Chris and comments on how they think our season went. Well, we all love and miss you. Stay safe and keep in touch.
   Love,
   Dacia, Randy & Justin ;-)

West bank of the Tigris River, Baghdad, 2105 Hours Charlie +1, Friday, 23Apr2004
   I heard the bullets whiz by before I heard the tat-tat-tat-tat-tat of the machine gun. It was dark now and I could see the tracer rounds coming from the other side of the Tigris River. As I heard the bullets impact the concrete wall of the empty building behind us I yelled "HIT THE DIRT"

and all 20 of us dropped as though we HAD been shot. Someone then yelled, "Lay FLAT!" The machine gun fired maybe 20 to 40 more rounds before it fell silent. Since we were all on an evening hash run, none of us had body armor or even a gun to shoot back. Since it was dark and the gunner was in downtown Baghdad it would have been tough to target him anyway without endangering innocent civilians. Nevertheless once the shooting stopped we got up and hurled a few choice words in that general direction. Now that the party was over we dusted ourselves off and walked back to take a shower and watch the late news, chalking up the experience to our luck holding out another day in Baghdad. In the past two weeks sources say that 595 U.S. soldiers have been wounded, raising the total number of wounded in combat to 3,864 since the start of the war a year ago.

Green Zone, Baghdad, 2254 Hours Charlie +1, Tuesday, 27Apr2004

Dear Mary,

Nothing new in Baghdad so far today (that's always good news). Been busy trying to get caught up and be ready in case they do decide they have a new mission for me and a few others. There haven't even been any mortar strikes nearby in the past week. Now I can't sleep because I am used to waiting for the first mortar strike before I sleep and it doesn't come. It is rare to see an airplane over Baghdad as there is no regular commercial air service. At dinner this evening I saw two F-16s circling high above. So I know they are on standby for something that is or will be going on. We'll see. The checkpoints are busy and Iraqis are back at work here again. I hope that doesn't change too much.

We have a new post office detachment opening up in a bombed out palace in the Green Zone that is closer to our unit than the one 15 miles away at North Camp Victory. For future mail, you can send to me at my new zip code (only the last number has changed):   SSG Dave Conklin, 350 CA COM, Baghdad, Iraq, APO AE 09348
Love you,
Dave

Baghdad, Iraq, 1200 Hours Charlie +1, Friday, 30Apr2004

Today is the last day of April and time to reflect on all the Americans who put their lives on the line. Below are excerpts from a USA Today story (Zoroya, 2004, p. 1):

Iraq's Deadliest Month

To the war's supporters, they are the face of freedom. To the war's critics, they are an unnecessary price of conflict. What made this month so deadly is the return of full-scale combat in which U.S. troops are being attacked by organized groups of insurgents in cities such as Baghdad and Fallujah.

The statistics offer a partial portrait of April's casualties: 117 men, 2 women, 15 more people whose names and genders have not yet been disclosed by the Pentagon. They come from all branches of the military. Their median age is 23. Active-duty troops outnumber National Guardsmen and reservists by about 5 to 1. The casualties include teenagers barely out of high school, like Marine PFC Dustin "Dusty" Sekula, 18, of Edinburg, Texas, whose mother signed papers allowing him to enlist at 17. He died April 1.

The two oldest were SGM Michael Stack, 48, of Lake City, S.C., and Chief Warrant Officer Patrick Kordsmeier, 49, of North Little Rock. Stack was a Green Beret, a father of six, grandfather of three and was nicknamed "No Slack Billy Jack Stack." Kordsmeier was a member of the Arkansas Army National Guard. Some who died had just arrived in Iraq. But then there was Army SPC Scott Larson Jr., 22, of Houston, killed in combat April 5, two weeks before he was due to go home on furlough.

Army SGT Felix Del Greco, 22, of Simsbury, Conn., was a former Eagle Scout who enlisted in the National Guard when he was 17. He used to tell a friend about his plans to run for president in 2024. "A soldier at age 17. A leader at age 22. He was the all-American kid from next door," Connecticut Gov. John Rowland said at his funeral. Del Greco died April 9.

April's death toll of 134 (as of 8 p.m. ET Thursday) was tallied from the Pentagon's daily casualty update; 119 names have been released. But the numbers are dwarfed when compared to the Vietnam War, during which the deadliest month was May 1968, when 2,478 U.S. troops died. Military analysts say the spike in casualties is because insurgents are learning how to attack U.S. troops and because the attacks are occurring during a period of transition, when fresh troops are coming into the country.

The Marines had high casualties this month because much of the 1st Marine Expeditionary Force arrived and was assigned an area that includes Fallujah and Ramadi, where guerillas are most active. In an e-mailed letter to Marine families sent from Iraq, the unit commander, LTC Paul Kennedy, said the violence in April was the worst the unit had faced in 30 years. "Within the blink of an eye the situation went from relatively calm to a raging storm," he wrote about the fighting April 6 in Ramadi. "The men we lost were taken within the very opening minutes of the violence. They could not have foreseen the treachery of the enemy and they did not suffer. We can never replace these Marines and sailors but they will fight on with us in spirit." At least five of the men who died had wives who are pregnant; 36 men were fathers. At least 60 children, from infant to adult, lost a parent.

Two female soldiers were killed in Iraq this month. Army SPC Michelle Witmer, 20, of New Berlin, Wis., died April 10, a day after her Humvee was attacked in Baghdad. Her two sisters, including her identical twin, were also serving in Iraq with the National Guard. Both said this week that they would accept the Army's recommendation that they not return to Iraq. Army Spc. Tyanna Avery-Felder, 22, of Bridgeport, Conn., was killed April 7 by a roadside bomb in Mosul. The Army had the most casualties of any U.S. military service in April, followed by the Marines. But there were also three sailors killed, and Air Force Airman 1st Class Antoine Holt, 20, of Kennesaw, Ga., died when a mortar round hit his tent at an airfield in Balad.

Every branch of the American military was represented in April's death toll. Bruckenthal of the Coast Guard died from injuries suffered in an explosion. He and U.S. Navy personnel were preparing to board a dhow that was approaching an oil terminal in the northern Persian Gulf. As they neared the small craft in an inflatable boat, the dhow — in what was believed to be a suicide attack — blew up. Two sailors also died. April's war dead came from 38 of the 50 states. And some were from U.S. territories: Navy Petty Officer 3rd Class Fernando Mendez-Aceves, 27, of Ponce, Puerto Rico, was killed April 6 in Ramadi. Army SGT Yihjyh Chen, 31, of Saipan, Northern Mariana Islands, died two days earlier in Baghdad fighting.

One irony of the conflict in Iraq, where soldiers can so readily call families from battle zones, was that on more than one occasion in April, wives who spoke to their husband one day learned within 24 hours that they were dead.

This happened to Beatriz Carballo, 18, who spoke with her husband, Army SPC Adolf Carballo, 20, of Houston on April 10, the Saturday morning before Easter. "He didn't sound like he was saying goodbye," she says about the conversation. "He was just sad because he was not home." Her husband said it was evening in Iraq, and he had a mission scheduled after dinner. The next morning, Easter Sunday, Army officers arrived at her door. Carballo had died from shrapnel wounds in an explosion in Baghdad. She was stunned.

U.S. fallen troops during April, 2004:
Men: 117, Women: 2
Median age: 23, Youngest: 18, Oldest: 49
Active duty: 101, Guard/ Reserve: 18
Army: 64, Marines: 50, Navy: 3, Air Force: 1, Coast Guard: 1
Officers: 10

6. The Desert Heats Up

Green Zone Café, Baghdad, 1248 Hours Charlie +1, Tuesday, 04May2004

I woke up Monday with a stomach flu that's been going around and now I have diarrhea and a queasy stomach. I slept for 12 hours yesterday and should have done the same today. It kept getting worse and I progressively got weaker and more dehydrated from not wanting to eat much and from the constant diarrhea. But I try to go to every meal to keep my strength up. I had lunch today at the CPA Presidential Palace and was feeling bad on my walk back. As I was crossing the street I heard a loud "CRACK" further up the street towards the hospital. I stopped for a few seconds in case there might be more, but hearing none I figured it was another mortar strike and so finished my walk back to the finance building.

Forgetting the incident I was already back at work mentioning how bad I was feeling, when 1LT Gary Drozdowski, the disbursing officer, burst into the room and hollers, "I'm NEVER going outside this building again! Somebody just threw a grenade at me!" The L-T and SGT Greer, both from the 136th Finance Company offices upstairs, had walked two blocks north past the Ibn Sina 31st Combat Support Hospital to the corner "Green Zone" Café for lunch. Near the hospital an Iraqi work crew had moved in to begin hauling away piles of rubble and to reconstruct an apartment building next to the street. On the way back from lunch as they walked by the empty building the L-T says he saw something go over his head and hit the street. He continued,

> "As it bounced I saw it was a grenade and yelled GET DOWN. As I lay there I remember looking right at the grenade and it still had the spoon on it! I was thinking, 'it's a dud!' – Then POW it went off and put holes in parked cars, broke windows and sprayed shrapnel in every direction – except ours!"

By some miracle no one was injured and the L-T and sergeant got up and walked VERY FAST back to the building and called Force Protection who sent troops to cordon off the area and search, without success, for the worker who threw the grenade. The episode again reminded me that there is no safe haven here in Baghdad, even in the Green Zone. A number of questions come to mind. Who did it? No one knows which laborers LIKE us, and which ones want to KILL us! Where did the grenade come from?

Was it smuggled in the back of a dump truck full of dirt, or stolen from a careless GI whose Humvee was parked along the street? What would I have done in that situation? Would I have jumped up, locked and loaded and tried to chase down the assailant—or run for safety like the L-T? Some questions are better left unanswered.

SSG Dave Conklin, from Kalispell, Montana, a public affairs specialist with the 350th Civil Affairs Command takes photos with a new friend on Haifa street between the CPA Presidential Palace and the 31st Combat Support Hospital in the Green Zone, Baghdad, Friday May 16, 2004. (Baghdad40) (Photo -- Dave Conklin)

Denver, Colorado, 0916 Hours Tango +1, Thursday, 06May2004
The sister of my former Montana National Guard commander writes:

Hello David,
I am Major Nikki Dewolf's sister. She has been forwarding your e-mails to me. I want you to know how much I enjoy them. I get so tired of listening to the news & their viewpoints of the war. I take every opportunity to speak in support of the efforts that are going on overseas. My church has a group that prays regularly for our troops & any one in specific that we may know. I will be adding your name to our prayer list & the name of your unit if you are allowed to provide that. If you have anyone else you would like us to add to that list or specific prayer requests, please forward them on to me, I will make sure the prayer warriors of my church will get that info. I am attaching a picture of Nikki, Me & our other sisters Gina & Jan. This picture was taken last year at my 30-year class reunion icebreaker at Hap's. I was going through Chemo treatments when this picture was taken. I am now done & have a full head of short curly hair. Well I had better get back to work. May God bless you & protect you!!

Julie Sassano Robbins

Julie:
Thanks for the message, and the great photo! If you are at all like your sister you must be a great person too! Nikki was my commander when I was in the 111th Press Camp in Helena. I am now part of the 350th Civil Affairs Command, a reserve unit that commands all the civil affairs battalions here in Iraq. You can send my stories to anyone you want, and all of us could use your prayers here.

   I would ask that you also pray for all the soldiers who are at increased risk because of the actions of a few in their less than human treatment of prisoners at the Abu Graib Prison here last year. Their actions will ultimately result in the deaths of more Americans, as they only help the enemy grow stronger. Good soldiers and citizens should be incensed by what they did. In the meantime, God bless you and everyone back home, as you are the only reason we are here. I hope I can meet you someday when I return.
SSG Dave Conklin
350 CA COM
Baghdad, Iraq
APO AE 09348

Baghdad, Iraq, 0845 Hours Charlie +1, Saturday, 08May2004
   By now, a full year after the fall of Baghdad, we had all hoped that we would be helping rebuild Iraq's schools, water, sewer, and electrical systems, and training government agencies and private businessmen on how to run their country. Instead we are raiding schools and Mosques for hidden weapons, conducting full-scale combat, and trying to prevent the car bombing, kidnapping, ransoming, and even be-heading of private businessmen. Attending a daily threat briefing quickly dispels any thoughts that Baghdad has been getting any safer lately. Here are some notes of interest from today's 8:45 a.m. daily CPA Deputy Chief of Staff meeting:

   -Zarkawi Group has claimed responsibility for the VBIED (i.e. car bomb) Explosion at 14th of July Bridge Checkpoint last Thursday, May 6th.

-The risk of the possible use of VBIEDs at checkpoints and areas around the "Green Zone" still remains high.
-BIAP shuttle was attacked yesterday at 0910, a vehicle in the convoy was hit by an IED (Improvised Explosive Device) and one KBR contractor was killed.
-There were 44 attacks on Coalition Forces yesterday resulting in 0 KIA and 17 WIA.
-Anti-Coalition Forces (ACF) are shifting focus toward Baghdad. Baghdad Region has become the most active for attacks with most being IED and VBIED.
-In Southern Iraq ACF are planning to kidnap individuals driving "Soft cars" such as non-hardened SUVs driven by CF.
-Possibility for an emergency accountability drill today.
-Mother's Day is this Sunday 9 May.

A view of the site of a car bomb explosion at the 14 July Bridge Checkpoint at the south entrance to the U.S.-led Coalition Provisional Authority (CPA) headquarters in Baghdad. (cp11 car bomb) (Photo -- AFP/ Ramzi Haidar)

We also get a printed threat update by e-mail based on zones within Baghdad as well as regionally in Iraq:

-UNCLASSIFIED-
DAILY CPA OPERATIONAL THREAT UPDATE: 06 MAY 2004
BAGHDAD THREAT CONDITIONS:
Zones 9, 17, 18, 21, 28, 30, 31, 51, 54 and 90 are Red. Use all security precautions if entering these zones. Do not travel there unless you have urgent business.
Zones 1, 5S, 8S, 12, 16, 19, 20, 22, 23, 24, 26, 36S, 37S, 40, 52, and 72 are considered uncertain. Use all security procedures if traveling there.

Zone 26:   SAF Attk; CF (Coalition Forces) reported that assailants driving a Red Daewoo and Blue Daewoo shot at a FPS guards.
Zone 23:   Izs (Iraqis) Detained; CF stopped and detained 3xIZs, at a TCP along a HWY, in a dump truck containing 100+x 60mm mrt rds (mortar rounds).
Zone 20:   Mrt Rds; An ICDC (Iraqi Civil Defense Corps) bunker was attk w/ several mrt impacts. ICDC reported seeing the spotter on an adjacent building's rooftop; the spotter and 3x other males left the building and fled on a Silver BMW. 3xIZs were detained.
OUT REGIONS:
S. Cent: Al Hillah; IED Attk; A CF convoy was attk w/ an IED ambush. The IP informed CF they have detained 2x suspects.
Diwaniyah; Cache Found; CFs searched a girl's school. The school was suspected of having a weapons cache on its grounds. Hidden behind a makeshift wall CFs found a 60mm mrt tube and tripod, 10x RPG rnds, and 20x 60mm rnds. Unit will follow up w/ a civil affairs team to instruct locals that such practices will not be tolerated and it puts the students at risk.
Mahmudiyah; IED Attk; IRR reported an explosion on the railroad line damaging an engine. The train dropped its load of concrete bunkers and reached Mahmudiyah.
South. E: Al Qurnah; Hostile Crowd; A CF patrol stopped 3x IZs suspected of being highway robbers. They had in their possession a light machine gun and 2x AK-47s. While making the arrest, around 200x IZs gathered at the scene and were acting very hostile, threatening the patrol to release the detainees. The patrol threw 2x smoke grenades and withdrew taking the confiscated weapons and leaving the 3x detainees.
Basrah; Train Accident; CFs reported a train accident. Reports from the scene would indicate the junction had been tampered with. ICDC elements are securing the scene.
Safwan; Detainees; CFs acting on information received from the ICDC/IP arrested 6x personnel vic of the border crossing point at Safwan. In addition they confiscated 3x AK-47s w/ 8x magazines, 70x rnds and 6x Kuwaiti license plates.

Baghdad, Iraq, 2200 Hours Charlie +1, Wednesday, 12May2004

A little while ago this evening gunfire broke out on all sides of the green zone. For about half an hour I watched tracer rounds arching high in the sky, as well as green, red, and white parachute flares. I could hear automatic weapons and small arms firing at irregular intervals. I watched it from our roof and tried to take some photos while listening to spent shells landing nearby. I wasn't sure who was attacking whom except that the whole thing reminded me a bit of Independence Day fireworks at home. Later I heard on BBC radio that, "gunfire was heard in Baghdad after the Iraqi football team won their match against rival Saudi Arabia to qualify for the summer Olympics." They had to play in Amman, Jordan of course because it was too dangerous to have a soccer game here in Baghdad. It's quiet now so I think I will go to bed.

Looking west from Baghdad's Green Zone late Wednesday night as tracer bullets arc through the sky celebrating Iraq's Olympic soccer team upset over Saudi Arabia to qualify for the summer Olympics in a gritty, come-from-behind victory. May 12, 2004. (P8210080) (Photo --Dave Conklin)

Baghdad, Iraq, 0916 Hours Charlie +1, Thursday, 13May2004

Today I am working on a contract for building Interrogation Facilities for the BCCF (Baghdad Coalition Correctional Facility), better known as Abu Graib Prison. Photos of prisoner abuse there have caused Congress to hold hearings on what went so terribly wrong. One of the things that I heard while I have been in Iraq was that many soldiers are not being held accountable for their actions.

This may change soon for some according to a May 6th story in the Washington Post (Washington Post, 2004):

The Abu Graib Story
The photographs appear to provide further visual evidence of the chaos and unprofessionalism at the prison detailed in a report

by Army MG Antonio M. Taguba. They were taken by several digital cameras and loaded onto compact discs, which circulated among soldiers in the 372nd Military Police Company, an Army Reserve unit based in Cresaptown, Md. The pictures were among those seized by military investigators probing conditions at the prison, a source close to the unit said. The investigation has led to charges being filed against six soldiers from the 372nd. "The allegations of abuse were substantiated by detailed witness statements and the discovery of extremely graphic photographic evidence," Taguba's report states. For many units serving in Iraq, digital cameras are pervasive and yet another example of how technology has transformed the way troops communicate with relatives back home. From Basra to Baghdad, they e-mail pictures home. Some soldiers, including those in the 372nd, even packed video cameras along with their rifles and Kevlar helmets.

All I can say is that it's hard for me to believe that U.S. soldiers would abuse Iraqi prisoners then take photos of it to prove they are guilty. It's hard for me to believe that U.S. soldiers would commit acts that border on treason and will surely lead to the deaths of their fellow Americans. It's hard for me to believe that U.S. soldiers from a Military Police unit could claim that they had never been trained on the provisions of the Geneva Convention. It's hard for me to believe that U.S. soldiers would say they had been ordered to violate the rights of POWs and then go ahead and do it anyway. It's hard for me to believe that U.S. soldiers would be court-martialed without their officers who permitted all of this to happen. It's hard for me to believe that U.S. soldiers would be so stupid and so careless with their actions that they would discredit a whole army, a whole nation, and a whole war. But I guess maybe I came from a different army, a different nation, and a different war.

Denver, Colorado, 0916 Hours Tango +1, Friday, 14May2004

Today I received an e-mail from the church pastor of my former commander's sister Julie who wrote me earlier this month. I felt good that there were still folks who do support those of us who are trying to do the right thing.

Hello David,
You don't know me but I am on staff at Crossroads Church of Denver in Wheatridge, Colorado. Julie Robbins Sassano forwarded your e-mail to me and your prayer requests have been placed on our Bless Our Military prayer list. I personally want to thank you for your sacrifice you have made for citizens such as myself and my family in the name of freedom. My support for you and all of the troops across the world is prayer and these efforts with the prayer list. This list is picked up by some prayer warriors in our church. I know at times maybe your spirits are down and I hope in some way this e-mail passes some encouragement to you. No matter what we are going through the Cross will never be moved or fall. Keep your focus on that Cross and know there are many here in the United States who support you and are in prayer for you and the leaders of our great country.
In Christ's Service,
Bob Newell
Pastoral Care Administrative Assistant
Crossroads Church of Denver

Al Quadisiyah District, Baghdad, 1225 Hours Charlie +1, Monday, 17May2004

As soon as we came around the corner in our two white Toyota Pathfinders the traffic slowed to a complete stop with Iraqi drivers on all sides of us. I was sure that SFC Chapple driving behind me was ready to pee his pants. Even though we were locked and loaded and I had an MP-5 on my lap and a 9mm pistol on the floor, being in a Baghdad traffic jam is not a casual affair lately. But he kept his cool and as soon as I spied a break in the traffic, I turned into the oncoming lane, drove through the intersection and we soon reached the airport highway, the route we intended to take in the first place.

Today we are taking MSG Arnette Robinson to BIAP (Baghdad International Airport) so she could fly back to her unit at Eglin Air Force Base in Florida, but our usual checkpoint out of the Green Zone was closed. Two hours earlier a suicide car-bomber had blown up himself and 9 others here—including Izzadine Saleem the head of the Iraqi Governing Council who was in the last car of a council convoy. All other exits from the Green Zone would require us to drive through the streets of Baghdad and find our way back to the airport highway. I opted for driving down the Tigris River levee to the truck only gate. Since we were military the guards let us through. Then I had hoped to get on the highway that went over the river bridge but there were no on-ramps.

So we meandered through the streets of the Al Quadisiya District, passing stores, open vegetable markets, apartments --and plenty of traffic. The best protection we have on our trips is maneuver and camouflage. Here we lost our speed, but not our ability to blend in—at least we weren't in the Humvees that are so easily recognizable by any bad guys who might be in the vicinity. The Iraqi drivers next to us in the traffic were quite surprised to see us . . . but not enough to get out of our way!

The rest of the trip to BIAP and then Camp Victory went as planned, but then we had to return. I called ahead and was told that the checkpoint that had the car bomb was still closed so we decided to go back the way we came. We left Camp Victory and on the highway passed a lot of traffic to include a Bradley and an M1 tank going the same direction. I decided to drive to the closed checkpoint anyway to get an update on the situation from the guards as I could always backtrack to an open checkpoint. As luck would have it they let us drive through the roadblock! After we parked and unloaded our weapons and cars and congratulated ourselves on a mostly uneventful trip, Tec SGT Birkland came out of our building and told us that soldiers had found an IED near the airport road that had nerve gas in it—another new danger to add to the mix. Our next trip is on Wednesday. I hope the checkpoint is open by then.

Sergeant Daniel Palmer stands in front of his ASV (Armored Security Vehicle) across the street from the Ibn Sina Hospital in Baghdad, Iraq. Sergeant Palmer from Butte, Montana, is an MP with the 66th Military Police Company from Fort Lewis, Washington. His unit is currently stationed in the ancient city of Babylon. Sunday May 23, 2004. (DCP02300) (Photo --Dave Conklin)

7. Approaching the Speed of Sovereignty

Near the Presidential Palace, Baghdad, 0605 Hours Charlie +1, Saturday, 05Jun2004

The mortar impacted outside my window at precisely 6:05 a.m. I didn't know where exactly, but it was close enough to rattle the window and wake me up, which means it was less than a thousand yards. I wondered if this was going to be one of those "non-routine" days. It turned out to be just that. Again I was in charge of our 2-vehicle convoy to the Baghdad Airport today to take SFC Chapple, one of our NCOs, to catch a flight to Kuwait. Yesterday I arranged to spend some time on a makeshift rifle range at nearby Forward Operating Base (FOB) Highlander. Three of us were able to practice with M16s, AK-47s, and MP-5 assault rifles. So now we knew for sure how they would shoot—and we found that about one out of every twenty Iraqi-made 7.52mm cartridges would jam in our Kalashnikovs but the Egyptian-made ammo was OK. We were ready for another convoy.

After more detours, construction, and slow-moving convoys we delivered SFC Chapple to the airport, delivered postcards to the post office, and stopped at the new Burger King and PX at North Camp Victory. Afterwards we delivered a dozen boxes of communications equipment to the 57th Signal Battalion at South Camp Victory. It was 5:07 p.m. and the temperature was about 99 F when we locked and loaded for the trip back to the Green Zone. Riding shotgun with me this time was our Iraqi interpreter Moyaad Razzook (the one from Houston, Texas), who wanted to come along today only to visit the new PX. I gave him my M16 and kept the MP-5 on my lap. In the chase car was SSG Babin and Specialist Nelson, my new officemates on loan from the 2nd Brigade, 1st Cavalry Division. I wasted no time on the way back, driving 120 to 140 kilometers per hour with windows open, guns ready, swerving under bridges to avoid hand grenades, watching for IEDs, and watching other cars for possible rifles or RPGs as we sped along.

Moyaad asked if I would slow down when we reached the burned out Chevys again so he could get a picture with his camera. Just as I said NO, the traffic in front began to slow anyway, and then I could see cars and trucks turning around and coming back towards us. Something was definitely wrong. I thought it might be another military roadblock as I could see a flatbed cargo truck stalled in the center lane, a small car with its windows broken blocking the right lane, and some Humvees ahead. As soon as we slowed I heard the "POP, POP, POP, POP, POP" of rifle fire to my left, then on my right. We had just driven into the kill zone at the same location of today's earlier attack. There were buildings, people, cars, and even goats all around. It was impossible to tell where the shots were coming from, or even to return fire without injuring a bystander. But I had one hand on the MP-5 if a target could be found. "GET DOWN!" Moyaad said, but how do you get down when you are the one driving?

As I pulled up alongside the flatbed truck for cover, several Iraqi men from the truck and car who were also caught in the crossfire began diving for cover next to their vehicles. The man on my left had blood streaming down his right arm. I wish I could have helped him but they motioned for us to go on. They knew they would be safer with us far away from them! I maneuvered through the narrow space between the wrecked car and truck and checked my mirror as I sped off to see if our chase car had been hit. SSG Babin's white Toyota soon appeared out of the wreckage and two miles later we came through Checkpoint 12 behind the 1st Cavalry Humvees that had just run the same gauntlet.

After we reached the office Moyaad got his picture–in a "safer" location. Then we cleared our weapons and took off our helmets and body armor. SSG Babin quipped, "Back there when you heard them shooting I was afraid you were slowing down to take their picture!" The news media reported on today's events as follows:

> Iraq's new prime minister, in his first televised address to the nation, called for a halt to attacks on Americans and other foreign soldiers, saying their presence would be needed to help the sovereign leadership improve security. Also three people died in an ambush on the road to Baghdad airport on Saturday afternoon and a U.S. soldier was killed and three others wounded in a bomb attack as bloodshed continued in the run-up to the June 30 handover deadline. The U.S. military said the three ambush victims, believed to be contractors, were shot dead by assailants who opened fire on their two-vehicle convoy from several directions with Kalashnikovs. The bodies of the three victims were ripped apart and charred, said one U.S. officer. Trails of blood trickled along the tree-lined central reservation, and body parts had been wrapped in a black bag (Associated Press, 2004).

U.S. Army forces secure the scene of attack, where two vehicles were destroyed on the airport highway, in southern Baghdad, June 5, 2004. A group headed by suspected al Qaeda operative Abu Musab Al Zarqawi claimed responsibility for an attack on two cars of the type favored by Westerners in Iraq, saying it had targeted 'CIA' agents. (r1949288151) (Photo -- Reuters/ Ceerwan Aziz)

Joint Contracting and Finance Office, Baghdad, 1225 Hours Charlie +1, Wednesday, 09Jun2004

I write home that I'm still alive and kicking though having a bad case of diarrhea for the first two weeks of May then two more weeks with a chest cold. I was finally feeling better; then my convoy was ambushed last Saturday, but we sustained no injuries. It is interesting to see how people from different services and past experiences react differently to daily threat briefs, mortar attacks, and convoy ambushes!

Now I'm trying to catch up on work and writing as well. I am buying everything from sandbags to armored vehicles for the troops here. I think it is almost summer here too as the temperature is now over 100 F every day. Body armor only feels good AFTER you take it off, and I have to wear Nomex fire resistant gloves to keep from burning my hands on the door handles and steering wheels.

The office operation here has a lot of similarities to my previous tour in Bulgaria. We have 3 translators, 2 Army and 1 Air Force Administrative Clerks, and 3 contracting officers: 1 Army MSG, 1 Air Force MSgt, 1 Navy LCDR female supply officer, and scores of Iraqi, Saudi, Turkish, Lebanese, and other private businessmen and women who want to sell us things.

Presidential Palace, Baghdad, 1330 Hours Charlie +1, Thursday, 10Jun2004

I had heard that there was a room full of Saddam's and Uday's treasures somewhere in the basement of the Palace. At the end of the north hall I found the office of Air Force Major Aaron Benson, Deputy Facilities

Manager for CPA. Displayed in glass cases along the walls of the room was a small selection gold and silver plates, urns, swords, and other museum pieces—including a 1960 Oregon car license plate.

When I asked him about it, Major Benson gave me a story written by Timothy Noah. It goes like this: A 1964 movie called *The Yellow Rolls Royce* tells the story of three successive owners of the same luxury vehicle. Perhaps it's time for a remake called *The 1960 Chrysler DeSoto*. It would tell the story of one automobile's 40-year journey from Oregon to the main presidential palace in Baghdad. As a person with the web name "Chatterbox" reported in December 2003, a license plate with the tag number 2Z-351 turned up, heavily caked with dust, in one of Saddam Hussein's many garages. Although quite obviously not high on anyone's list of priorities, the plate and how it got there is a mystery to the U.S. Army. When Chatterbox attempted and failed to trace the plate through the Oregon DMV he was told it wasn't in the computerized files.

Unsatisfied with this outcome several media outlets had Oregon DMV spokesman David House look up the Oregon plate in the written records. House determined that the plate was attached to a 1960 DeSoto whose registration expired in December 1983. Many sharp-eyed readers pointed out to Chatterbox that the plate's design and its "Pacific Wonderland" motto were a dead giveaway that the plate was issued in the 1950s or 1960s.

Apparently Chatterbox could have learned this himself by logging onto www.oregonplates.com. The plate also has an "84" annual sticker in the upper right corner which is still a mystery. House further determined that the owner of this 1960 DeSoto was one Richard Foley, who informed the Oregon DMV in December 1987 that he had sold the car prior to 1985. "There's no way," said House, "to know when the car and the plate were separated from each other after December 1983." House also found that on Foley's last Oregon driver's license, which expired in 1997, he listed his residence as Seaside, Ore., in the state's northwest corner.

Upon learning all this, a nationally syndicated radio program called *The Lars Larson Show* (produced by KXL News Radio in Portland) asked its listeners if anyone knew of a Richard Foley from Oregon who owned a 1960 DeSoto in the early 1980s. This apparently turned up a young man named Rick Foley who said the man in question was his father, who is currently serving time in Duluth Federal Prison Camp. Chatterbox has not yet reached Rick Foley, and so can't confirm that this is true. He has, however, requested an interview with the Richard Foley at the Minnesota prison. And there our story, for the moment, ends.

An Oregon license plate, tag number 2Z-351 with an "84" annual sticker and the motto "Pacific Wonderland" is part of the Saddam and Uday collection of the Facilities Management Office in the Coalition Provisional Authority Presidential Palace, Thursday June 10, 2004. (Image001)(Photo -- CPA)

Republic Bridge over the Tigris River, Baghdad, 0800 Hours Charlie +1, Monday, 14Jun2004

The war here in Iraq has been brought closer to home than any other because of technology. Not only are cable TV networks beaming live news feeds all over the world, but also soldiers themselves are in touch real-time with their friends and families using everything from cell phones and digital cameras, to web cameras on laptop computers. This morning was, unfortunately, a perfect example. I was using my cell phone and a calling card given to me by the VFW to call my wife Mary for our weekly chat and also to wish her a Happy Birthday. As I was talking I heard a BOOM outside our building. I took the cell phone with me as I went out to investigate, describing to Mary what was happening and what I heard and saw. As I rounded the building I could see a large cloud of smoke rising from less than a mile to the northeast. Just then the siren went off at the CPA. She could hear it, real time, from where she was in Kalispell Montana at 10 p.m. that Sunday night.

I explained to her that I didn't know what the boom was yet, but that I thought it was loud enough to be the headline TV story on the Monday morning news. Later that day I found out I was right. It turned out to be one of two car bombings in Baghdad that killed more than 20 people in less than 24 hours. This one was just across the river from us on Tahrir Square, one of Baghdad's most crowded traffic circles and a choke point for traffic. A parked car, filled with up to 1000 pounds of explosives was detonated, killing 12 and injuring 60, Iraqis and Americans both. The blast was aimed at a convoy of GE engineers in Toyota Land Cruisers like the ones we drive. It also destroyed a dozen cars and damaged a whole city block. Mangled burned-out car frames and small pieces of body parts remained for all to see.

Two Iraqi men stand next to the mangled frame of one of the Toyota Land Cruisers that were the target of a car bomb that killed 12, including several General Electric contractors Monday, June 14, 2004. (IMG2639) (Photo -- Moyaad Razzook)

Also a 120mm rocket hit the CPA Presidential Palace about 11:00 a.m. the day before. Up until now, the palace had been blessed by near misses. Luckily, the rocket caused no casualties, except for the lady that fainted when she saw the windows break nearby. I'm only glad I was too busy to get my hair cut at the CPA barbershop yesterday.

Riverside Compound, Green Zone, Baghdad, 0830 Hours Charlie +1, Tuesday, 15Jun2004

I found there are three things we can count on in Baghdad: the sky will be blue, the days will be hot, and the violence will escalate. In fact ambushes, assassinations, and car bombings have been escalating steadily since the beginning of June. Today I needed to get to Camp Victory again. The Camp is located 10 miles west of the Green Zone on the airport highway designated as "Route Irish." But U.S. soldiers know this section of highway better as "ambush alley." The escalating danger of coordinated ambushes by Jordanian militant Abu Musab Al Zarqawi's agents with RPGs, IEDs, and small arms has caused me to change travel methods as well for the time being. Instead of SUVs, I am now riding in up-armored model M114 Humvees with crew-served weapons.

Sergeant Kevin Evans, from Plainview Texas, with the 350th Civil Affairs, is the lead driver on a Humvee convoy returning from Camp Victory west of Baghdad to the Green Zone on Route Irish. This 10-mile section of highway is better known to soldiers as "ambush alley" because of the constant danger of attack by RPGs, IEDs, and small arms fire from abandoned buildings and bridges such as this one. Tuesday, June 15, 2004. (DCP02386) (Photo --Dave Conklin)

The June 5th SUV attack on this highway was a well-coordinated ambush. Yesterday's IED attack across the river was also aimed at SUVs that were traveling through a choke point. The bad guys are looking for "soft" targets if they can find them. Today is no different. As soon as we leave Checkpoint 12 and pick up speed, Specialist Don Sanders from Crestview, Florida, in the navigator seat relays a radio message that Route Irish has just gone "Red." This is the Force Protection Office's code for "avoid if at all possible." Sure enough in a few minutes we pass a foot patrol of 1st Cavalry soldiers, then we come to a roadblock—near the same location as our June 5th ambush. Humvees and M2 Bradleys have sealed off the westbound lanes after an IED was found. Once again I get to detour across the median and into the eastbound oncoming traffic. This time an Iraqi in an old red Nissan almost sees us too late and just makes it into the other lane, nearly rolling his car with a too sharp turn. After another detour for a second IED, we arrive at Camp Victory.

The return trip went a little faster and smoother—and hotter. By 4 p.m. when we arrived back at Riverside Compound, the little thermometer I carry on the outside of my body armor was maxed out at 50C (120F). Our gunner, Sergeant Mark Mayer from Panama City, Florida, said his watch thermometer only registered 112F. This is always the best part of the day though, because I get to take off 45 pounds of body armor, helmet, weapons, magazine pouches, and camelback pack. Not only does it lighten my overall body weight by about one-third, but also both my DCUs and underclothes are so damp from sweat that I actually feel cool for a while—until I change and go for my daily 2-mile run!

Riverside Compound, Green Zone, Baghdad, 0900 Hours Charlie +1, Thursday, 17Jun2004

Today I had another trip to make to Camp Victory to work with the folks at the Third Corps Comptrollers Office, or C-8. I didn't get much sleep last night. At 12:30 a.m. there was a mortar attack, then at 5:30 a.m. a multiple rocket attack nearby rattled the windows. Now, just as I was putting on my helmet and getting into the Humvee, I heard another "ka-BOOM" to the north.

I found out later that an SUV loaded with artillery shells was driven into a crowd of people waiting to volunteer for the Iraqi military, killing at least 35 people and wounding 138. It happened at the same ICDC recruiting center near the Muthanna airport that I saw the explosion kill 47 people last February 11th and was the deadliest incident since then. It was the third suicide car-bombing just this week in Baghdad and the 16th this month in Iraq. We are now reaching a point of having a car bombing every day as Al Zarqawi's terror network tries out a new tactic of simpler, more frequent car bombings to shake confidence in Iraqi security forces ahead of the handover of country sovereignty. Lack of security here affects every aspect of making Iraq a free and stable country. Sabotaging oil pipelines, killing contractors who are repairing electric generators, and assassinating Iraqi government officials outside their homes are great ways to keep Iraq in chaos and its people in poverty.

Iraqi security walk past a man inspecting the body of a victim following a car bomb outside the army recruitment center in Baghdad Thursday, June 17, 2004 (25725) (Photo -- AFP/ Ahmed Fadaam)

I deal directly with a lot of local Iraqi businessmen here. One of our contractors who among other things has a contract to pick up garbage was behind in his pick-ups. When I called him I found out that one of his drivers was shot and killed to intimidate the others not to work for the U.S. Last Tuesday his truck convoy from Jordan was ambushed. When the bad guys found out that the goods were for U.S. Army customers, they lined up his six Iraqi drivers along the side of the road and executed them.

Yesterday I spoke with SFC Ferguson, our Civil Affairs guy at the Ministry of the Interior who works with Iraqi General Saad at the CPA. He said, "Just yesterday I shook hands with the general, and this morning he was assassinated outside his home." Most of the violence here has been terrorists against Iraqis who want freedom and democracy.

Green Zone, Baghdad, 2326 Hours Charlie +1, Friday, 18Jun2004
My retired Army Attaché friend in Washington D.C. writes:

> Is it just me or does anyone else find it absolutely amazing that the U.S. government can track a cow born in Canada almost three years ago, right to the stall where she sleeps in the state of Washington, and determine exactly what that cow ate. They can also track her calves right to their stalls, and tell you what kind of feed they ate. But they are unable to locate 11 million illegal aliens wandering around in their country, including people that are trying to blow up important structures in the U.S. My solution is to give every illegal alien a cow as soon as they enter the country. –John Dooley

Interesting proposition I think. So I send it on to my other friends for comment. My National Guard Colonel friend writes back:

> See Dave, the farmer has to register the cow when they are born and track them through their life cycle to reap the benefits of the farmer/rancher subsidies paid by the government to them. The terrorist and illegal immigrant don't have to register when they come in the country 'cause there ain't no cash incentive. All we need to do is get a bunch a Southern bubbas, give 'em a trailer on the border, arm them with a scoped .30-06, and give 'em a bucket of bullets and free Friday barbeque and beer, with a $10 "heart or head" bonus and I triple damn guarantee you there wouldn't be any illegals gettin' in. The ACLU and Concerned Citizens for a Borderless United States might get a little pissed but there wouldn't be any illegals either. Hey life's a series of tradeoffs. As an added incentive if the illegal gets past the bubbas they get to go to the top of the citizenship line with no waiting period and a giant economy sized bottle of Coca Cola --I like a "win-win" situation. --Pete

Presidential Palace, Green Zone, 0830 Hours Charlie +1, Monday, 21Jun2004

Lieutenant Commander Woody Brown, one of my Hash House Harrier friends who works for the CPA is kind enough to forward the latest threat briefings to us as well as general CPA news. Here is a typical addendum to the daily threat brief:

> VEHICLE SEARCH REMINDER
>
> CPA employees are reminded of the importance of searching their vehicles for Improvised Explosive Devices (IED). Recent events have shown that insurgent forces have targeted and are likely to try to place IEDs on coalition vehicles. Leaders must ensure that all vehicles under their command are searched on a regular basis and prior to use, regardless of where the vehicles are parked. This includes vehicles that are parked in the Green Zone. PSDs are also reminded of the need to ensure positive control is retained over all vehicles entering the Red Zone. If a vehicle must be left unattended in the Red Zone, even in a "secure" site, it must be searched prior to use.

By reading this message I can tell that a civilian State Department "weenie" working at the CPA wrote it. Now if III Corps put it out, an Army Captain would have been assigned to write it and to show off his outstanding grasp of Army "intelligence," he would have shortened the message into only one sentence by using every military acronym that he knew, and sent it in all capitals in message format:

06210530Z2004
ATTENTION: CPA GIS AND NGOS MUST CHECK THEIR NTVS FOR IEDS DURING PMCS AS PER SOP BECAUSE ACFS ARE TARGETING CF SUVS AND NTVS BY PLACING VIEDS ON CVS EVEN IN THE GZ; THEREFORE PSDS MUST ALSO MAINTAIN C2 OVER CVS IN THE RZ AND SEARCH FOR IEDS PRIOR TO DEP.

Steel Dragon Staging Area, Green Zone, Baghdad, 1705 Hours Charlie +1, Friday, 25Jun2004

"Get away from the luggage," barks a sergeant as I get out of my car. Under the tin-roofed awning at the shuttle bus stop are three rows of duffle bags, suitcases, and backpacks. A German Shepard leaps out from a cage in the back of a black Chevy Suburban. His handler carefully takes him up and down each row of bags as he sniffs for signs of explosives. Soon the sergeant with the K-9 MP armband shouts, "all clear" and 30 people move in to claim their bags.

One of them is Laura Poitras from New York and the director of the documentary *"Flag Wars."* (Poitras. 2004). Today she tells me she is working for Praxis Films on a new documentary *"My Country, My Country,"* about life for Iraqis under U.S. occupation (Poitras. 2006). Laura says the film will include the work civil affairs soldiers are doing with Iraqi civilians to rebuild the country and prepare for elections in January 2005. She says her first task is to film Baghdad in the days immediately before and after the government hand-off, then film civil affairs soldiers in the field working on governance and reconstruction.

My task, in addition to my current job, is to fill in for two other public affairs soldiers who are on R&R leave. One of those was supposed to be her escort. Now, according to BG Davidson, I am. She is lucky to arrive today, as this may be one of the last shuttles from the airport since all Coalition forces are being put on alert and restricted to "mission essential" travel until after at least July 4th. She recognizes my nametag, as I only know her name, and that from a couple of e-mail messages. Luckily she is traveling relatively light and has the newer lighter digital video equipment. She also has a black body armor vest and helmet that she bought for the trip.

I lock her bags in my SUV and since we are at the Presidential Palace, suggest I get her a visitor pass and we have dinner there before I take her to her room at the 350th's heavily guarded Riverside Compound. Inside the palace we stop at C9 CMO (Civil Military Operations), to leave my M16 and body armor as this is the only dining hall that bans rifles. 1LT Cooper, General Davidson's aide-de-camp, is there and sets up an impromptu dinner with the General and a couple of his staff. After we talk about the project, plans are made for filming the unclassified portion of the staff briefing the next morning.

Riverside Compound, Green Zone, Baghdad, 1117 Hours Charlie +1, Sunday, 27Jun2004

The first day I think I was an excellent media escort for Ms. Poitras. As for the second day...Well, you be the judge. We were just walking away from the 350th headquarters when we heard the first rocket. As we turned back toward the building it exploded about 250 meters away. Laura threw herself to the ground, camera pack and all, wedged in between a Humvee and the building. I crouched over her, just in case the next one was closer. Luckily the second rocket was a dud. While we stayed there motionless for a minute or so I heard someone yell, "I hate this shit!" I picked her up, dusted her off, and said, "Welcome to Baghdad." I could see she was rattled by the new reality of being in a combat zone. Luckily the rockets landed in a vacant lot and damaged only parked cars and building walls, rather than people this time. Then she said, "You weren't joking when you told me yesterday that people call you 'dangerous Dave' because you attract hostile fire."

Our next stop was the Iraqi Convention Center, or IAC. This afternoon U.S. Ambassador Paul Bremer was giving a farewell talk to some of his Iraqi staff and Ms. Poitras wanted to film it if possible. As we walked by another large conference room, out came the new Iraqi Prime Minister Iyad Allawi with a half-dozen bodyguards and another dozen or so aides. Standing there in uniform with an M16 I could only think fast enough in Arabic to say *"Marhaba"* (Hello), to which he replied, *"Ahlen Wa Sehlen"* (Welcome). We finally found the room where the meeting was to be and I left her with the newsroom escort from the CPA. Two hours later

I got a frantic call. She told me that the bomb-sniffing dogs had knocked her camera over and broke it before she could film anything—on the second day of a month-long trip. Luckily my friend Staff Sergeant Singleton, a 25-Romeo video technician, works at the Coalition Press Information Center. By the time I arrived, he had glued the lens back together so that the camera would work until Fed Ex could deliver a new one from New York. It was a bad day, but she made the best of it, saying, "I still have two days to plan my shots for the day of the transfer." Wanna bet?

8. A New Government is Born

Joint Contracting and Finance Office, Baghdad, 2211 Hours Charlie +1, Friday, 09Jul2004

This evening I finally feel well enough after a second bout with the flu to write thank you notes for a couple of care packages:

Mary,

I've still got the flu bug, malaria, or whatever, but it's moving around and I am feeling good enough to type and go outside into the sauna-like temperatures of 120 F these days. Thanks again for the sweet care package with my favorite newspapers and fig bars as well as the lifesavers, hot chocolate and mint goodies. I just hope I get well enough soon to have a bigger appetite so I can eat them faster.

It's been quiet here in the Green Zone for the past 2 weeks, but the fighting and killing are not far away. We had 5 killed and 20 wounded just yesterday in Samarra when they fired 40 mortars into the compound there. It is riskier for them to shoot here as we are a much larger target area and they have to shoot from downtown. Let's hope it stays quiet!

As for R&R leave, they are saying I will leave here on 21 July, which puts me into Dallas or Atlanta probably on 22 July with arrival in Kalispell probably on 23 July. I am allowed 15 days to be back in Dallas or Atlanta so that means leave Kalispell probably on 5 August, and get back here about 7 August. Hope that helps your planning.

I Love you much and can't wait to see you again! --Dave

Carolyn Blashek & SSG Elizabeth Cowie,

I was one of the soldiers who was fortunate enough to receive an Operation Gratitude package last week. I wish I could shake the hand of every person and every organization that contributed to this but since I can't, please pass along my deepest thanks to all as best you can, especially Emma whose flag, picture and message I will keep here with me. In return I'll attach a recent photo of me.

Recently I have been slowed down by the flu bug, malaria, or whatever, but now I am feeling good enough to go outside into the

sauna-like temperatures of 120 F again. Everything is appreciated and I will share this package with other soldiers as they do with me. I just hope I get well enough soon to have a bigger appetite so I can eat the treats faster.
    Thanks again.
SSG Dave Conklin
350th Civil Affairs Command
Baghdad, Iraq
APO AE 09348

Rich:
Thanks for the great care package! It came at the end of last week but I was too sick to pick it up until yesterday. It was well-wrapped as usual and I know John Domenech got his too because we picked them up at the same time! I started passing things around as soon as I opened the package and I guarantee you it all disappeared in no time at all. Unfortunately I could not write until now because I had the flu, malaria, or something--again. The young Army doctor at the hospital thinks it's the flu and gave me some Motrin, but if it doesn't go away soon I'm going to demand more tests. Thanks for everything Rich. You're a true patriot of the highest order.
I'll keep in touch. --Dave

From : Rich Pylypuw
Hi, Dave. Wow, sorry you've had such a tough time. Drink a hell of a lot of water, even if you don't feel you need to. It flushes crap out of your system and heals the body.
    Thank you for the kind words. Glad to send stuff over. It's the easy part to do that. Dave, you are the true patriot. Guys like you who volunteer don't have to be there, but are in answer to the call of duty. You chose to put yourself at risk and sacrifice the good life for a while to do a job that needed to be done by someone. It's different than the ones who are mobilized and didn't particularly want to go. That's how it was when I joined up with that unit to go to the Gulf War. However, it was a really screwed up outfit. Bad leadership and undisciplined troops, with very few exceptions. No wonder they weren't up to strength and needed volunteers. You are in a completely different kind of unit and working with

professionals, which should make for a very rewarding experience for you.

That should have been the second package, the one with the book. I hope you enjoy it. It's a fascinating read. I sent number three out on July 2nd, last Friday. Still haven't figured out a good way to send over the fun stuff. U.S.P.S. has all these signs about prohibited items, liquids and such, which can't be sent parcel post. I think I could package it up real well so that nothing would leak out even if the box got mangled, but you never know. I hate to screw somebody up. I'm still giving it lots of thought.

Are you going to be able to get an R&R to come home for a bit? They've had some MT ARNG guys that have done that already. I hope you can. A year in the sandbox without a break is a long time. As for me, things are really a grind. I have no life. It's either work, which is busy; school, which is busy; or Rotary, which is busy. No time to work on the house, which would also keep me busy, or anything else. I'm behind in everything, especially school. It really gets depressing, sometimes, to think that's all there is. And I'm not getting any younger. Still looking for a change of some sort.

Drill is this weekend. We have weapons qualification and I am a team leader, the only M-day guy. What that means is that when we have to clean weapons on Sunday, all the full-time people will have an excuse not to do it and I won't be able to do anything about it. Like a straw boss, no authority over them. I'm getting tired of the Guard, too, but need to hang in there another 3 - 1/2 years to the very end. It goes by quick, though.

Well, Dave, I hope you get to feeling better. And tell John to use his connections to get you promoted. That still is disappointing and not right.

Hang in there, my friend. --Rich

Rich,

Thanks for the newsy letter. Hey I really appreciate the book you sent, and the articles too! As I am writing about Iraq I really want to put things in perspective and hear from other sources so those are some of the best things you could have sent!

Don't worry about sending any liquid. Believe it or not some Iraqi guy (must be a Christian) opened up a liquor store here in the Green Zone! I can't buy any, but my Christian Iraqi linguist can! Hey! I got some things I want to send you and I lost your address! Please send it to me and I'll send a reverse care package--still trying to figure how to bottle up some dirt from the Tigris River for you too.

The good news is that I am about 95% better now and trying slowly to get back into shape, but for some reason my joints are real sore. What a weird flu virus I have. I hope it goes away completely soon. The other good news is that they put me on the R&R list for the end of the month so I should be getting a free ride home for a couple of weeks. If I can't see you, I will at least give you a call to see what's up.

Good luck with all the stuff you are into this summer. I know you will push through and get it all done. I think I can identify with your "no life" comment. I also have a friend who is now with a company that manages a lot of the computer simulations for the Army both here and elsewhere. As soon as I find out more about it, I'll let you know in case you are ready for a change when you are done this summer or fall. We'll see. Don't forget to send me your address.

Thanks again, --Dave

Checkpoint 2, Green Zone, Baghdad, 0915 Hours Charlie +1, Wednesday, 14Jul2004

Although the war was all around us in Mosul, Tikrit, Balad, Baquba, Fallujah, and Ramadi, it had been unusually quiet in central Baghdad since sovereignty had been transferred to the interim Iraqi government on June 28th. But I was worried about when and how the peace would be broken.

The answer came out of the clear blue sky at 9:15 a.m. The loud BOOM reminded our four Air Force newbies who had only been in country for a few days that their 90-day tours were indeed in a war zone. As they scrambled to get their body armor from upstairs in their rooms, the finance troops scrambled down the stairs to the ground floor which also serves as our "bomb shelter." I grabbed my IBA and Kevlar helmet from the chair next to me and headed upstairs to the roof for a better look.

At first I thought a mortar had landed close by, but after the first cloud of dust-colored smoke drifted off, I could see another cloud of black smoke rising from the vicinity of the Al Rasheed Checkpoint. I had seen that color of smoke before—from burning vehicles and car bombs. I knew people would be dead. I only hoped that the death toll would be low.

Black smoke rises from a car bomb attack at Checkpoint #2 near the Al Rasheed Hotel and the entrance to the Green Zone in Baghdad. According to interim Iraqi Prime Minister Ayad Allawi, 10 people were killed and 40 wounded in the attack. Wednesday, July 14, 2004. (DCP02463) (Photo --Dave Conklin)

The blast occurred on a national holiday marking the 46th anniversary of the bloody nationalist coup that killed Iraq's last king, Faisal II. News reports later said the blast killed 4 Iraqi Civil Defense Corps soldiers, 7 Iraqis waiting in line to apply for jobs with the new government, and maimed another 40 people, including one American soldier. The estimated 1000 pounds of explosives made a crater in the pavement 3 feet deep and 6 feet wide. Some say it was a suicide bomb meant to retaliate for Tuesday's Iraqi Police sweep that arrested 500 militants in Baghdad. It was the worst attack in Baghdad since the June 28th car bombing.

Our linguist Moyaad had just returned from picking up another linguist at this checkpoint only 3 minutes before the blast. He is scheduled to go home to the U.S. for a month off beginning Friday. I think he is long past ready for a break. Especially since all this is happening against the latest hostage threats and beheadings of Bulgarian truck drivers and Filipino workers. I'm afraid that our new Air Force folks who are not used to all this carnage might have difficulty sleeping tonight.

Ad-Diwaniyah, Iraq, 0915 Hours Charlie +1, Friday, 16Jul2004

There's an old saying that goes "a bird in hand is worth two in the bush." But what do you do with more than a dozen Barn Owl chicks handed to you in a war zone? Here in central Iraq as well as elsewhere in the country, U.S. Army Civil Affairs teams under our command are helping to provide the initial civilian expertise needed to reestablish government services and economic stability for industry, agriculture and animal husbandry. Recently they proved again that no challenge is too great and any task worth doing is worth doing well.

The story begins during the last week of May at Camp Scania, a Convoy Support Center near Ad-Diwaniyah, about 80 miles south of Baghdad. Local workers were dismantling an abandoned batch plant for asphalt and concrete when they discovered a Barn Owl nest with eight baby owls. The Barn Owl, Latin name *Tyto alba*, is rare and declining in numbers throughout its range. It commonly nests in abandoned buildings in settled areas and is one of nature's best mousetraps, but is rarely seen because it hunts exclusively at night. It is also one of the easiest owls to identify with its heart-shaped facial disk.

Unfortunately, one of the ancient beliefs that still hold sway here is that owls are regarded as "death omens" and are killed whenever they are found. The workers threw the nest and the owl chicks to the ground. Luckily soldiers from the 1-185 Armor Battalion found two chicks still alive and brought them to SGT James Bourdon, a combat engineer from Mission Beach, Calif. who is working with our Civil Affairs team at Camp Scania.

"They were young Barn Owls still covered with down with signs of their feathers developing," said SGT Bourdon, also a former volunteer at a wildlife rehabilitation center. "The older owl suffered from a broken leg," Bourdon continued. "I tried to look in the phone book for vets or pet stores but then I realized there was no phone book or phones for that matter and I was in an Army camp in Iraq," he said. While SGT Bourdon began hydrating the owls with a plastic syringe, the team notified LTC Kevin Carr, the Civil Affairs liaison officer at Tallil Air Base near An-Nasiriyah in southern Iraq who began contacting other civil affairs experts on diet and care.

CPT Thamus Morgan, a veterinarian with the 415th Civil Affairs Battalion in Tikrit, Iraq e-mailed Professor Mark Pokras at Tufts University and found that owls should be fed pieces of small rodents if possible--meat, hair, bones and all. Meanwhile LTC John Maxwell, the Food and Agriculture Team Chief with the 416th Civil Affairs Battalion in Mosul, Iraq contacted Dr. Steve Marks, the director of the Elmwood Park Zoo near Norristown, Pa. who provided recommendations on splinting the older owl's leg. An Iraqi veterinarian in Ad-Diwaniyah administered antibiotics and splinted the broken leg.

Success was mixed. Another owl nest with six more even younger baby chicks was found and destroyed by the workers. SGT Bourdon took these chicks in also, becoming both mother and drill sergeant for his now eight-member "*Al-Booma* squad" as he called them. *Booma* is the Arabic word for owl. Bourdon did what he could. "From a plastic syringe I was able to get all the owls to drink water and got them to eat whole sardines from cans I bought at the PX." Despite his best efforts, the oldest owl with the broken leg soon died and by late June the Al-Booma squad had been reduced to a single remaining chick from the first nest, now named "Tyto" (tie-toe) after the Latin name for Barn Owl.

In the meantime from Tallil Air Base LTC Carr coordinated with COL Robert Anderson and LTC John Hustleby in Camp Doha, Kuwait to locate a wildlife rehabilitation center that could raise and "hack" or teach the now feathered owl to fly and hunt on its own. On June 25th LTC Hustleby and SPC Jessica Fano with the 350th Civil Affairs Command team in Kuwait finished making the final arrangements for Tyto's new life. Even coalition partner Japan agreed to help by providing military air transport. "Tyto made the convoy trip to Tallil Air Base on my lap," said SGT Bourdon. Then he made his first flight—in a C-130 cargo plane to Kuwait.

Once in Kuwait, Tyto first visited Dr. Natasha, a raptor specialist at the International Veterinary Hospital in Kuwait City who examined the owl and pronounced it healthy. Soon COL Adamson relayed the plan for Tyto. "After the owl spends a couple of days at the veterinary hospital getting the proper nutritional diet and vitamins, we are moving it to the

Scientific Center in Kuwait where it will live with a variety of other birds and be well taken care of."

Kuwait's Scientific Center, on the coast of the Arabian Sea at As-Salimiya, was built in 1996 as an initiative of the Emir of Kuwait and the Kuwait Foundation for the Advancement of Science (website: www.tsck.org.kw). Not only does the Center have the largest aquarium in the Middle East, but also a desert section dedicated to preserving rare wildlife of the Arabian Peninsula, including Barn Owls.

LTC Hustleby recently checked on Tyto's progress at the center and reported, "He has grown considerably. They are training him to fly from one point to another and there is still a possibility that he will be released back into the wild." In the meantime, SGT Bourdon in Scania and LTC Carr in Tallil are keeping their fingers crossed that Tyto, now on the Who's Who list of Barn Owls, will someday be flying the wide-open skies of Iraq and the Arabian Gulf—without the need for a cargo plane.

Sergeant James Bourdon from Mission Beach, Calif. with the 1-185 Armor Battalion Civil Affairs team prepares Tyto, the surviving Barn Owl chick for his first flight—in a Japanese Military C-130 cargo plane. Bourdon raised Tyto and several other chicks from two destroyed nests for nearly a month by scrounging everything from mice to meat scraps. Tallil Air Base, Iraq. Friday Jun 25, 2004. (SGT Bourdon) (Photo -- SPC Jessica Fano).

Joint Contracting and Finance Office, Baghdad, 0930 Hours Charlie +1, Friday, 23 Jul 2004
As I prepare requests for bids here in the Joint Contracting Office, I come across an e-mail from my friend Keith at BIAP who is looking for a buyer

for some armored cars. I haven't priced any lately but his e-mail convinced me that we won't be replacing our Toyotas any time soon:

7/23/2004

Alcon,

One of my suppliers has informed me of three each Toyota Land Cruisers Level B6 and B7 that were Built and flown to Baghdad. All Units are new 2004

2 of the vehicles are equipped with the 4.7 liter V8 engine and all the luxury components normally associated with this model: protection level-B6

1 of the units is equipped with the 4.2 TDIC (diesel) engine, all the bells & whistles also but protected to the higher B7 level.

Individual price per unit will be USD $168,000.

If interested, drop me a line or give me a call.

V/r
Keith T
Country Manager
Saudi Naval Support Company Ltd.

9. Summer in the City

Hartsfield Atlanta Airport, Georgia, 1400 Hours Bravo +1, Sunday, 08Aug2004

 Today was the end of my 15-day R&R leave back home in Montana. I said goodbye again to my wife Mary at 6:00 a.m. and took the first flight out of Kalispell stopping in Salt Lake City and arriving in Atlanta eight hours later at 2 p.m. as ordered. As I got off the plane from Salt Lake City I noticed another soldier in his DCUs with a Wyoming National Guard Patch on his left sleeve. Specialist Hicks told me he was from Casper and was also stationed in Baghdad. We found the Air Mobility Command (AMC) ticket counter, checked in, and were told to wait in line with the other 250 soldiers also going our way. Finally at about 3:30 p.m. they started issuing boarding passes for the flight at 8 pm. We finally got our boarding passes at 6:30 p.m. and then went to the food court for some pizza.

 Even here at the Atlanta airport where there were a lot of soldiers in uniform several strangers greeted me with "Thanks for your service" and "where are you from? and going?" One lady who thanked me was a Canadian from Toronto. Unlike in Baghdad, I was pleased that I didn't have to carry a gun here to feel safe in a uniform. Later, on the charter plane, some of the soldiers were talking about where they went and what they did on leave. I overheard the sergeant behind me say, "As soon as I got off the plane my girlfriend and I made love right in the parking lot at O'Hare Airport. She said she was going to make love to me so much that it would be six months before I would get an erection again."

Mary greets Dave on his arrival at Glacier Airport for two weeks of R&R (rest and recuperation) leave from Iraq. Friday, July 23, 2004. (Photo --Dave Conklin)

Frankfurt, Germany, 1100 Hours Bravo +1, Monday, 09Aug2004

The sky was clear but hazy as our charter DC10 flew over the patchwork quilt of farm fields, woodlots, and villages of whitewashed houses with red roofs on our decent to Rhine-Mein Air Base near Frankfurt. At the terminal, Chaplain (MAJ) Young of the 1st Infantry Division greeted all 250 of us who got on the plane in Atlanta with a handshake as he did on our stop here three weeks ago. After the obligatory briefing we were allowed to use the phones, bathroom, food court, and AAFES store at the terminal. Sergeant Jared Shumate from my unit, who spent his entire R&R with a missionary in Moldova, came up and said hi. Then after refueling we were ready for the 4 1/2 hour flight to Kuwait.

By the time we circled the lights of Kuwait City and landed at the airport at 8 p.m. it was dark. The pilot spoke over the intercom and said the temperature here was 42 degrees. I thought, "That's not too bad." Then I remembered, "That's Celsius. Oh no! That's 106 degrees Fahrenheit." A baggage detail was appointed and after loading bags and soldiers our 5-bus convoy and Humvee escort arrived at Camp Doha after 30 minutes. No time for sleep though.

As soon as I started breathing the air, I got a tickle in my throat and my nose began to clog up from the dust and pollen. No wonder. Camp Doha is located outside of Kuwait City, right next to a power plant with four huge smokestacks. The first time I saw their smoke plumes in the sky I thought they were large jet contrails or thin clouds—until I saw the source. Specialist Madden of the 847th Personnel Services Battalion was our "tour guide." He is a reservist from Ohio and said he arrived a month ago after being put on active duty with only a week's notice. Madden said an average of 600 soldiers and marines going on R&R come through Camp Doha every day. A few days ago an Omni Air charter plane broke down and over 1000 service members were stacked up here. In the customs room I saw a brass Saddam Hussein head and asked Madden about it. He said they found it in a crate that a Marine unit had in their Conex container. They planned to sneak it out of the country as a war trophy but had to give it up.

We lined up with our bags in a tent as soon as we got off the buses. First we swiped our ID cards and went through the obligatory briefings again. "Welcome back, get your head back in the game, don't ignore your feelings, and stop drinking alcohol and start drinking water." Next we stood in line to retrieve our IBA and Kevlar helmets from large boxes in the warehouse. Finally we were released to take our gear to another warehouse full of bunkbeds and take a half-mile walk to the dining hall. We had a 2:30 a.m.

roll-call to get our flight times, then another 8 a.m. roll call. Finally at 9:30 a.m. we had roll call for 48 of us scheduled on "chock 2" to get on the buses for the 1-hour drive to Ali Al-Salem Air Base for our C-130 flight back to Baghdad at 2 p.m. Our female bus driver to the flight line was a young, obviously new, soldier. She drove us down the tarmac and across the sand to just about every C-130 with its ramp down until she finally found the one we were supposed to be on. Finally we loaded up for the hour and a half flight over Iraq to BIAP (Baghdad International Airport).

Sergeant Jared Shumate, 350th Civil Affairs Command, returning from two weeks of R&R searches for his body armor and helmet in a box marked "July 21, #6" at Camp Doha building #9 in Kuwait City Monday, August 10, 2004. (DCP02533) (Photo -- Dave Conklin)

Freedom Rest R&R Resort, Green Zone, Baghdad, 1730 Hours Charlie +1, Tuesday, 10Aug2004

After 60 hours on the "road" including 20 hours of actual flying time, I am back in Baghdad. I rode the armored shuttle bus from the airport with our new Chief of Contracting, Air Force COL David Glowacki, who is on a 120-day tour from the Pentagon. As soon as we picked up our bags, LCDR Acqavella said, "Jump in, we're on our way to Freedom Rest. They had a rocket attack last night. By the way, meet CPT Finch, one of our new contracting officers just in from Fort Lewis." SSG Babin chimed, "You missed all the fun. On Sunday your unit's Projects-5 apartment building burned down, and later we had so many mortars come down that we watched them from the roof. Then last night the rocket attack woke us all up again."

MSG Steve Foster at the Freedom Rest R&R facility showed us the third floor kitchen that now had a new window where the wall used to be. He said, "They probably launched the rocket from the top of that brown building next to the white one you can see over there across the river. See, here's where a can of V8 was embedded in the bedroom door; and the wall that separates the bedroom from the kitchen has a lot of cracks and bulges now," he said.

Apparently two female soldiers staying at the resort had just left the kitchen at about 11:23 p.m. after making a snack when it happened and luckily were only shaken up. I mentioned that this was the third or fourth time I recall that a mortar or rocket had landed on or near the resort. Can you believe they give soldiers in Balad, Mosul, and Tikrit who are subjected to daily mortar and rocket attacks a 4-day pass to come to the Green Zone to an R&R facility where they are subject to more mortar and rocket attacks?

We assessed the damage so that we could work up a statement of work for repairs. Then we took photos of the two swimming pools, checked out the tennis court, and had dinner on real porcelain plates before driving back to our office and quarters nearby. CPT Finch quipped, "Maybe they should change the name of the resort from Freedom Rest to Eternal Rest." Since I had major jet lag, I was hoping that tonight would be quiet enough for at least one night's rest.

Staff Sergeant Todd Babin, 3rd Brigade Combat Team, 1st Cavalry Division stands in the third floor kitchen of the Freedom Rest R&R Resort apartment in Baghdad's Green Zone where a rocket attack narrowly missed two soldiers late Monday night. Wednesday, August 11, 2004. (DCP02560) (Photo --Dave Conklin)

Baghdad, Iraq, 2130 Hours Charlie +1, Thursday, 12Aug2004

Tonight at about 9:30 p.m. we were watching TV in our break room when we heard the rapid staccato of automatic weapons in the distance. Airman Robertson, SSG Babin, and I went upstairs to the roof to investigate and were treated to a repeat performance of what we saw last May 12th. Tracer rounds were arching high in the sky from all sides of the International Zone with an occasional "ping, pang" as spent bullets hit objects on the ground around us. Shortly the Embassy PA system siren went off—with the announcement, "Do not be alarmed, this is only celebratory gunfire." I said the Iraqis must have won another soccer game. Today's AP news confirmed it:

> PATRAS, Greece - In its first Olympic competition since its country was shattered by war, Iraq upset star-studded Portugal 4-2 on Thursday in a gritty, come-from-behind victory that set off cheers and celebrations among some 200 fans. "This victory will be received with happiness by my people, who have suffered through much," said Iraqi coach Adnan Hamad, whose countrymen were already taking to the streets of Baghdad, lighting up the night sky with streaks of celebratory gunfire. The stunning victory over a team that made it to the finals of the recent Euro 2004 tournament brought a rare moment of joy for Iraqis plagued by violence, chaos and constant power outages.

Much later I was talking to a woman who worked for Titan, the company that we contract with for our local English-speaking Iraqi receptionists and linguists, including Nibras, Ragad, and Dr. Razzook. Titan operates out of the gold-domed gate near the old Ministry of Information. She said that night some of her colleagues went up to the dome to watch the tracer fire and coaxed a newly hired worker into going with them. He didn't want to go but they told him to put on a helmet and flak jacket and he would be safe, so he finally agreed. Then while they were watching the show a bullet pierced his boot and went between his big toe and second toe. She said he still walks with a limp.

FOB Steel Dragon, Green Zone, 1230 Hours Charlie +1, Friday, 13Aug2004

Today no one was celebrating. As I cleared my M16 rifle at the clearing barrels inside the gate to Forward Operating Base Steel Dragon, I could hear the sounds of a large crowd in the distance. I asked the soldier on guard who said, "They are outside Checkpoints 1 and 2 protesting the wounding of Moqtada Al Sadr and the siege on his militia in Najaf." August is shaping up to be another deadly month for the coalition. Already more than twenty American troops have lost their lives in combat. This is the 7th day of fighting in Najaf, whose name means "a high land." It is located 110 miles south of here on a desert plateau and is the third holiest city of Islam, following Mecca and Medina in Saudi Arabia. As of today more than 300 insurgents have been killed.

A lot of the fighting has been near the gold-domed shrine of Imam Ali bin Abi Talib, the cousin and son-in-law of the prophet Mohammed, who was killed and secretly buried here in 661. Shiites believe Adam, the biblical first man, is also buried here. Shiites also believe that it is a holy place for them to be buried. But the Sadr Militia has used the shrine, mosque, and cemetery for hiding men and weapons. This is not your average cemetery and that is why nearly 4,000 American and Iraqi troops including the 11th Marine Expeditionary Force and elements of the 1st Cavalry Division are involved in the fighting. Imagine the New Orleans cemetery with its raised tombs on a desert. Then expand it to about 5 square miles in size with nearly 5 million tombs and you get the picture of what the world's largest cemetery looks like (see my photo in Chapter 16, October 4, 2005).

Al Sadr, Al Zarqawi and people like them, want to create an Islamic international political and spiritual empire, despite what ordinary Iraqis and the secular Iraqi governing council want. They have no qualms about using holy shrines for hiding and tactics like beheadings and suicide bombings in their ruthlessness to succeed. I heard that Saad Ali, a grizzled Iraqi military veteran now part of a special unit working with the Americans near Qaim, said through an interpreter:

> The people of the area I can read their faces. They hate the American forces. Even pregnant women want to give birth earlier to fight you. The respect we show them they don't deserve. We should kill from every house one person and not be sad. We should kill from every house one man. The enemy is ruthless. We must be as ruthless.

Islam has been divided into the orthodox Sunni and minority Shiite sects since shortly after the death of the Prophet Muhammad, founder of the religion, in 632. Sunnis accepted Abu Bakr, the prophet's friend, to lead their international political and spiritual empire. But a small group, the *"shi'at Ali,"* or party of Ali, believed that blood was thicker than water, and followed the much younger Ali, Muhammad's son-in-law, who would eventually head the Islamic empire. In the 7th century Sunnis killed Ali's son and Muhammad's grandson, Hussein and his 72 companions on the nearby plains of Karbala. Hundreds of thousands of Shiites make the pilgrimage to Karbala each March to mark Hussein's death in emotional annual rituals at the Ashoura festival (see Chapter 4).

Militiamen loyal to Moqtada Al Sadr fire a mortar at U.S. Troops from the streets of Najaf. Wednesday, August 11, 2004. (Mortar) (Photo -- AP/ Ali Jasim)

Joint Contracting and Finance Office, Green Zone, 0700 Hours Charlie +1, Wednesday, 18Aug2004

I am almost back to my normal routine today. But then what's normal in a war zone? The alarm went off at 6:45 a.m. I got up and made my bed, consisting of straightening my sleeping bag that I drape over me since it's too hot to get in it. But I've learned that draping it over me keeps the malaria-carrying mosquitoes from biting. Next I check the new thermometer I brought from the states and see that it is 35 C (about 85 F) outside. I wash up in the bathroom down the hall before the finance people get back from PT, comb my thinning grey hair, and shave.

I am the first one to unlock the office as usual and I eat my breakfast of frosted flakes, boxed milk and orange juice in the day room watching the CBS evening news at 7:00 a.m. on TV via the satellite dish on our roof. I could go a half-mile down the street to the KBR (Kellogg, Brown, & Root) dining facility but I only do that when I'm craving sausage and eggs.

Today I grab the car keys, my M16 rifle, body armor, Kevlar helmet and my "man-purse" and head out the door. I have an 8:00 a.m. meeting with COL Mel Howry in the 350th Civil Affairs Command Headquarters in the Palace of the King of Jordan on the west bank of the Tigris River. I am on his Public Affairs Team and we are planning the final trips to collect "good news" stories from our civil affairs units operating in Iraq. I also have some questions on my project for tomorrow. I will be doing a story on the visit of the House Armed Services Committee to our unit. After the meeting I check the mailroom and score a care package full of sweets and treats from a National Guard friend in Montana.

At 9:00 a.m. I go to a building we call "the cabin" to continue my weekly Arabic language lessons with our interpreter Melad, because *"Yatakallam al-arabiya kallilum faqut"* (I speak Arabic a little only). This is also where the clandestine "Mosquito" Newspaper that reports on local anti-coalition street-talk is published. At 10:00 a.m. I go back to 350th CACOM headquarters and climb the stairs to the third floor G8 Resource Management Office where I work three mornings a week to input our commitments and expenditures using the dBCAS (database commitment and accounting system) into the Army's computerized standard finance system or STANFINS. Our unit has an OMA (operations and maintenance) account of $4.7 million, two CERP (Commander's Emergency Response Program) accounts of $776,000 and $850,000 of seized money, and an OHDACA (Overseas Humanitarian Disaster and Civil Aid) account of $7.1 million. It is these last two accounts that pay for most of the direct reconstruction work that our civil affairs teams do.

By now it is 11:30 a.m. and I am getting hungry. I get in my Toyota Land Cruiser seized earlier from Uday's garage and drive about a mile down the street, past the Contracting and Finance building where my other office is, to the U.S. Embassy Annex at the Presidential Palace. I walk across the street in a narrow path through the jersey barriers and concertina wire and show my new blue embassy pass to the Gurkha guard at the newly opened concrete guardhouse at the front gate. The south entrance is closed for construction so I walk into the main door of the palace showing my pass to another Gurkha. I turn right and walk down the hall to the dining room.

The lines are as long as I have ever seen them. The well-built black man in front of me dressed in civilian clothes with body armor is packing a 9mm pistol. He says there are new sub-contractors serving the meals and they don't know how to do it yet. I notice that the Filipinos in the white chef hats are gone from the serving line. We heard a muffled "ka-boom" somewhere in the distance. The black man works on a PSD (personal security detail) for one of the Iraqi ministers. He said he had two mortar strikes close to him where he was earlier today. "So I looked through my binoculars to see where the spotter was, and there he was, on a rooftop, looking at me through his binoculars."

After lunch I met COL Howry in the rotunda and we went into the STRATCOM media center across from Ambassador Negroponte's office to meet with the Public Affairs chief, Rear Admiral Slavonic, about getting some AFN and combat camera support for our trips to the civil affairs teams in the coming weeks.

At 2:00 p.m. I arrived back at the Contracting Office. About 15 Iraqi contractors were in the lobby waiting to go on a site visit with one of our other five contracting officers. I knew several of them and greeted them with the standard greeting *"ahlen wa sehlen, as-salam alekum"* (welcome, come in peace). Two of them had questions on one of my requests for quote and Nuha from Bariq Trading Company gave me a copy of a contract I had asked her for to find out why she hadn't been paid.

While I was gone LCDR Acqavella, the Chief Contracting Officer for Baghdad had put two new purchase requests on my desk. The first was a rush job to purchase six bunkers for my boss MAJ Dunne at the 350th Civil Affairs Command. I had done many of these so I typed up an RFQ (Request for Quote) and printed it out for our interpreter Nibras to post on the bulletin board for a 3-day advertising period. Then I e-mailed the RFQ to several Iraqi companies that I know make these, and also sent a copy to the Iraqi Business Center.org to post on their electronic bulletin board. The second purchase request was for office furniture for three general officers at the Embassy Annex. As usual it was submitted by a staff officer who hand wrote it and provided no specifications. So I set it aside to look up previous buys I had made for general officers before I prepared an RFQ.

It was now 3:00 p.m. and time to check my e-mail for incoming quotes and messages. I downloaded 6 quotes for some plasma TV screens I had bid out for the 1-161st Infantry Brigade (Washington National Guard) at FOB Highlander. Then I printed out messages from contractors in the U.S., London, and Kuwait who had not gotten paid yet. For these I had to research the files of contracting officers who have already redeployed back to the states. I downloaded invoices, found the files, e-mailed or called the S4 (logistics office) of the units to see if the goods had been delivered, then prepared a receiving report, signed it and took it and the invoice upstairs to finance to prepare and express mail a U.S. Treasury check.

By 5:30 p.m. we were all hungry and I could eat early too since this was my night off from "PT" as I only workout every other day when I can. The dining facility at FOB Steel Dragon down the street was now open so six of us hopped into the Toyota and drove to chow. After chow, we stopped by

"Sam's Blockbuster Video Store" on a back street in the Green Zone just to take a photo of the signs that seemed a bit out of place. Great buys on pirated DVDs though!

Sam's Blockbuster Video store in the International Zone where great buys can be had on pirated DVDs. From left: CPT Finch, SSG Spell, LCDR Acqavella, SSG Babin, SGT Nelson, Wednesday, August 18, 2004. (DCP02588) (Photo -- Dave Conklin)

350th Civil Affairs Command HQ, Riverside Compound, Green Zone, 1030 Hours Charlie +1, Thursday, 19Aug2004

It was a hot August day when Congressman Jeff Miller (R-FL) made good on a promise he made in Florida last January to the soldiers of the 350th Civil Affairs Command. He said he would see us during our deployment in Iraq. Sure enough, today Miller and five other members of the House Armed Services Committee made Baghdad their first stop during a Middle-East fact-finding trip. Besides Miller, the delegation included Adam Schiff (D-CA), John Boozman (R-AR), Tom Cole (R-OK), Jim Marshall (D-GA), and Madeline Bordallo (D-Guam). After flying from Jordan over the city of Fallujah in helicopters and arriving in Baghdad, the delegation met with BG Charles Davidson and our staff officers before being treated to lunch with the soldiers of the 350th Civil Affairs Command, the 478th, and 425th Civil Affairs Battalions. The 350th from Pensacola and the 478th from Perrine are Army Reserve units from the state of Florida. The 425th is from Santa Barbara, California.

The 350th is one of four Army Reserve command headquarters for 24 Civil Affairs battalions in 25 states. "Ninety-seven percent of the Army's Civil Affairs assets are in the Army Reserve," according to BG Davidson. In Iraq, the 350th oversees the operations of four Army Reserve battalions: The 415th from Kalamazoo, Michigan, the 416th from Norristown, Pennsylvania, the 425th from Santa Barbara, California, and the 478th from Perrine, Florida.

Civil Affairs teams are attached to larger military units to provide the initial civilian expertise needed in war-torn countries such as Iraq to rebuild their country's government, economy, public facilities and humanitarian services.

During the meeting Congressman Tom Cole from Oklahoma asked, "How do the Iraqi people perceive your efforts?" LTC Wilfredo Rosario, 478th Battalion Commander replied, "The reality is people love what we do here. It's all about trust. When we say we will build a hospital we build it!" Civil Affairs projects in Iraq have included everything from refugee camps to youth centers, hospitals, schools, banks, and date palm orchard restoration projects. But rebuilding Iraq costs more than money. According to MAJ Mark Black, a Civil Affairs reservist from San Marcos, Texas, "The key is working with civilian organizations." But working with civilian organizations during combat operations sometimes puts soldiers in harm's way. So far during this deployment twenty civil affairs soldiers have been wounded in action and one has made the supreme sacrifice. Congressman Jim Marshall from Georgia added, "What you do is incredibly important, and you don't get recognized enough for the contributions you make."

After a quick lunch with the soldiers that included local fresh-picked dates; the delegation, undaunted by a tightly packed schedule, Baghdad's 110-degree temperatures and the midday sun, was off to another briefing before traveling to six more countries. "We cannot thank you enough for what you do," said Congressman Miller. "I am greatly honored to have the 350th Civil Affairs Command in Pensacola."

Members of the House Armed Services Committee, including Rep. Jeff Miller (R-FL) (left) listen as BG Charles Davidson, commanding general of the 350th Civil Affairs Command, explains the role of civil affairs teams in providing public facilities, humanitarian and economic assistance to the government of Iraq in Baghdad Thursday Aug 19, 2004. (P8190030) (Photo --Dave Conklin)

Joint Contracting and Finance Office, Green Zone, 1055 Hours Charlie +1, Friday, 20Aug2004

I respond to a note from my scoutmaster friend and former Army Engineer Officer back home:

Paul,

Thanks for the note on the Freedom Rest apartment damage. It was a rocket that came in at an acute angle hitting the wall on the left center of the hole. By the way, the new Stryker vehicles the 2d ID has up north have a "fencelike" screen around them based on the chain-link idea that forces the RPG to detonate before it hits the vehicle. Thanks for the care package suggestion. Chocolate chip or oatmeal cookies are always appreciated! Keep me posted. Let me know how you are working that with USACE. Will you be recalled from retirement or what? Good luck. Hope your "kids" are supportive. They are great young men. Tell them hi for me.
Keep in touch.

Dave C.

Dave,
    Betsy is pissed. The boys are well, acting sad, but they tell me "at least we don't have to worry about you being home all by yourself." They'll both be in Missoula at the University by the end of the month. USACE is looking for civilians with military experience to be contract managers in both Iraq and Afghanistan. They asked me if I would go over as a GS-13 instead of as a Major. I haven't compared the money yet but I got the feeling they were more concerned about me getting 20 good years than anything else. They really kept hitting the "use your 10 years of military time towards a federal retirement" and forget the green suit stuff.
Paul

AND I write my youngest sister:

Lori:
    Did I thank you for the care package? It got here about the time I was going on leave. It is great, and folks here love the comedy calculator! I got the book and recipe book for dates too. That's great because I have to write an article on what our civil affairs unit is doing with the date orchards here. The dartboard, even the soap is perfect timing. I just ran out. The cookies are all gone already but luckily Mary sent me a cookie package also. They tell us that we will be out of here in October so don't send any mail after about Labor Day. Mary said she talked to you about getting you a check for rental repairs. Thanks for getting them going. I sure appreciate it. Say hi to Jimmy and the boys.
Love Dave

AND from my National Guard friend:

Hi, Dave.
    Glad you made it back okay. John's e-mail is: John.Swanson@sfor.int. Royal and I have been in touch with him this week. He found Royal a tour in Bosnia and he's pretty sure he's got one for me, too. However, it may not be with Royal. Anyway, we're working on the paperwork. Still iffy about a caretaker for my dogs, but

I think I'll be okay by the time any orders come. I've got most of my bills being paid electronically, now, which wasn't the case last fall. So, there will be just a few things that my sister will have to take care of and also the kitty cats, but it won't be a mess like before. This will be a six-month TTAD and we think we'll probably leave about the first part of October. Don't know much at this point. Gotta go. I just popped in the office to check e-mail. I have to get my stuff ready for Helena tomorrow. Royal and I are going to do some field work on the RV Park in the morning. Take care, Dave. And, thanks again for the great gifts. I really appreciate it.
Rich

Rich:
     Thanks for the information! Keep me posted on your Bosnia opportunity. The great news is that your care package was waiting for me when I got back also. I just had to get over to the mail room when it was open and get it! Thanks for all the tools--just what I need here! And for the chips and dips and even toothpicks! Perfect! You sure know how to pack because even the Fritos weren't crushed! The magazines, even the old Butte Standard newspaper is appreciated. It's kind of nice to see what makes news in my other real world. I'll be in touch Rich. Thanks again.
Dave C

Joint Contracting and Finance Office, Green Zone, 1330 Hours Charlie +1, Saturday, 21Aug2004

Jassim Al-Qayssi, owner of Bariq Trading Company, and his English-speaking assistant Nuha came in today with another copy of the office trailer contract I had been helping them with since June. They have done a lot of business with us and have been both reliable and honest (rare in these parts!) so I thought I would try to help them. Of course when you work for the government, anything you try to fix usually gets worse rather than better and this would prove to be no exception.

   This problem started last May after they had signed a government contract to deliver a $20,000 office trailer to KBR (Kellogg, Brown, and Root) in Karbala, about 200 miles south of Baghdad. On May 12th their driver was ambushed and killed and the trailer was taken to a police station in the Al-Latifiya Area of Baghdad. From there one Army 1LT J.M. saw the trailer and decided to take it along with his Task Force 2-6 Infantry military convoy to nearby Camp Gator. By June, when I had made contact with him, 1LT J.M. said they had moved out of their camp and the trailer was now under control of the 2-2 Marines at FOB St. Michael.

Memorandum by SSG Dave Conklin at the Baghdad Joint Contracting Office documenting office trailer wartime delivery issues, Wednesday July 13, 2004.

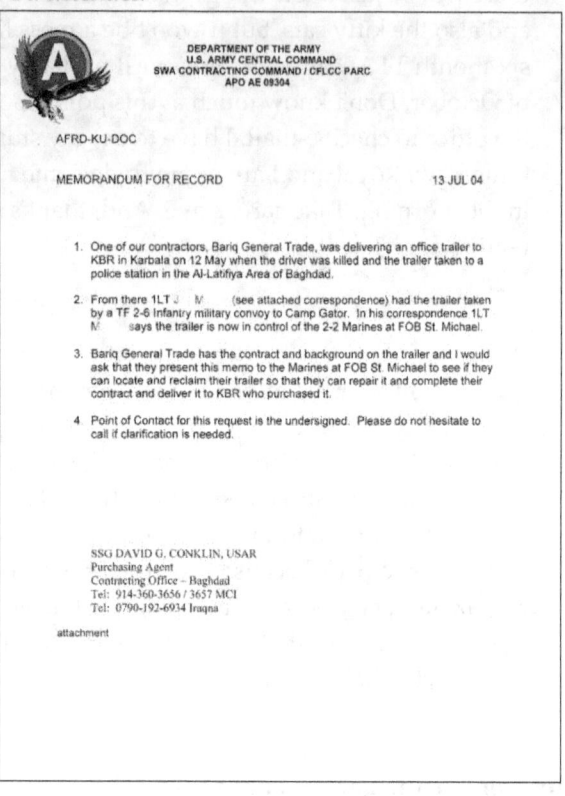

Since Bariq General Trade had the contract and background on the trailer, I wrote a memo for them to present to the Marines at FOB St. Michael to see if Bariq could locate and reclaim their trailer so that they could repair it and complete their contract and deliver it to KBR who purchased it. I thought that would be the end of it—but no. A Marine Captain e-mailed me to say that not only were they using the trailer, but that they had furnished it and had "built it into the wall" of their camp (which I can't even guess at how you would do that). So I suggested to the Captain that he simply fill out a purchase request and send it to his Marine contracting office and buy the trailer so that Bariq could then buy another one to fulfill their contract. This was in July, two months after the trailer was taken. Again I thought that would be the end of it—but no.

Now, a full month later after I return from R&R I get an e-mail message from a Marine Captain in the Ramadi contracting office telling the other Marine Captain at FOB St. Michael who is trying to do the right thing, that he can't write a contract because they didn't get three bids. Instead he says the contractor should file a claim for repayment (yeah, right—in whose lifetime) for this trailer that the U.S. government essentially took and won't give back. Battered but not beaten, I get another copy of the contract and buck all the correspondence up to the Chief of contracting in this office, LCDR Acqavella. She writes a pointed message to this Marine contracting officer, and gets basically the runaround. So she bucks it up to COL Glowacki out at Camp Victory, the new PARC (Principle Assistant Responsible for Contracting) for Iraq, who then tells this Marine in no uncertain terms to "buy the f**king trailer and get this vendor paid."

That was last week. Somehow I don't think I've heard the last of any of this. This week Nuha from Bariq Trading Company came by and said someone called her and threatened to kill her and her family if she didn't stop working for the Americans. She said she was going to live and work in Jordan for a while and would let us know when she returned. I told her I didn't blame her, wished her well, and told her to be careful.

Kalispell, Montana, 0826 Hours Tango +1, Monday, 23Aug2004
I opened my e-mail today to more news from home:
Dave,
Woke up this morning to screaming chickens. Our dog Risha and I zoomed (well she did while I hobbled side-ways) down the stairs. No fox but I knew it was somewhere. Checked the flock in the hen house . . . all looked at me and clucked. I went back inside . . . decided to open the upstairs window to let the breeze in . . . saw the neighbors black and white cat by the horse's feet in our neighbor's pasture and guess who came sneaking out of the machine shed??????

Mr. Red Fox, him/herself. I hobbled back down the stairs with our dog Risha. She zoomed again to the gate. I opened it but no fox. Risha started to sniff around and went into neighbor's corral and the kitty's big, black tail puffed straight in the air. I called Risha back to me. The cat turned out to be a skunk (in case you hadn't guessed) and came running straight at us. . . then it made a turn to the chicken coop and disappeared under the coop (scream!!!!!). I went out later and was missing a chick. Heard it peeping under the hen house. I finally came out and I caught it and put it back into the pen. When I went to find

where it got out and check the waterer I started to sink into a hole in the pen. There is excavation from Mr/Ms skunk under the dirt in the pen. I placed a piece of wire over the hole and Chris was to come over today but have not seen him.
Anyway, how is your day doing????
Love,
Mary

Mary:
   Well my day has been OK, but the Embassy has had its problems. It caught fire this morning. I opened my curtains at 7:00 a.m. and saw a black cloud of smoke. I thought they were burning trash--I guess not! It only affected a few rooms but the smoke was so thick that they cancelled lunch and dinner in the dining hall (back to MREs and salad)! Not only that but yesterday a mortar went through the roof and wounded two people on the third floor. Then of course the Iraqi soccer team won their semifinal heat in the Olympics and not only could I see the tracer rounds all around us Saturday night, but I could hear them falling on the roofs around us too. I only hope they win the tournament so they will expend all the ammunition they were saving to shoot at us. I'm sorry I forgot to call Sunday night. I am fine and will call and see if you are in during the week. Love you much,
Dave

Baghdad International Airport, 1400 Hours Charlie +1, Tuesday, 24Aug2004
My friend LTC William "Tony" Sobrero writes:

   Today Iraqi Airways landed their first airplane at Baghdad International Airport to restart their airline. I went over to take some pictures as the Boeing 737 taxied in. They had probably 100 people with several dignitaries to celebrate the arrival of the aircraft. They even had a group of new Iraqi Airways flight attendants. I was pretty surprised when a pickup drove up with five sheep in it. I was wondering what the sheep were for. Well, they dragged them out of the pickup and slit their throats and stuck their hands in the blood and made handprints on the aircraft, praise Allah! Apparently this ritual blesses a new possession. See the enclosed picture. I also have a picture of a motorcycle that was parked outside the palace. A Major was leaning on it talking on a cell phone after the Iraqi soccer team beat Australia at the Olympics and heard a thunk. The hole is a result of their celebratory fire. The sky was lit up with tracers, mostly going straight up. I hope they don't win a gold medal! --Paco (LTC William "Paco" Sobrero, MNF-I C3 Air Plans).

The inaugural flight of the first Iraqi Airways Boeing 737 to land at the Baghdad International Airport since the war is commemorated at a ceremony with bloody handprints made by sacrificing five sheep. (P8230008) (Photo -- LTC William Sobrero)

Karada District, Baghdad, 1025 Hours Charlie +1, Wednesday, 25Aug2004

Our convoy of five up-armored Humvees bristled with M249 machine guns sticking out of every top hatch, yet as soon as we stopped in the middle of Wazeer Street, the kids seemed to come from every alley, doorway and house in the Karada residential neighborhood. They were used to mobbing the soldiers of our Civil Affairs team because they knew we always had something for them. This time we had beanie babies donated by people all over the United States through our Beanie Babies for Baghdad website. I even opened two boxes of them myself sent from my hometown of Kalispell, Montana.

Today we were doing a media tour of Civil Affairs projects in the Karada district with AFN and FOX News video crews as well as the local Baghdad media in tow. Our first stop was the new Karada Youth Center. Here we stopped to chart the progress of the remodeling of a former residence of Saddam Hussein's brother-in-law into a youth center, including two computer rooms. According to Danny Hassig, an Army Reserve Major and sporting goods salesman back home and our 478th CA Battalion team leader for this district, the youth center was Safa Al Deen Hamzah Al Sultany's idea and passion. Mr. Safa is a district leader and now the manager of the youth center.

I had double-duty today. I was a journalist doing a story for our command to release, but while traveling in convoy I volunteered to be the M249 gunner on our up-armored Humvee. This can be one of the most dangerous jobs in a convoy, but it also has the best view. I soon learned that it also has some other drawbacks, the first being that while my buddies are sitting below with the air-conditioner blowing in their faces, I felt like someone set a giant blow-dryer on high and stuck it in front of my face. Sunglasses and Nomex gloves are a necessity. The second drawback I experienced a little bit later as the Humvee in front of us splashed through one of the occasional puddles of raw greenish-colored sewage and sprayed it into my face. On the other hand it was a nice clear day and the temperature was only about 116 degrees.

Our next stop was the Rasafa Health Center. We stopped in a long narrow side street just north of Omar Bin Yassif Street and walked a block past a butcher shop, fruit stand and grocery store to the clinic. As I walked I greeted the children and shopkeepers with the standard greeting: *sabah al-khair, as-salam alekum* (morning of light, peace be upon you). In turn I was greeted with a smile and *sabah an-nur, alekum as-salam* (morning of good, peace upon you). I felt that the people here really appreciated that we were trying to help them, unlike most of the TV and radio news I have heard recently. I was happy that the FOX News team was with us to do a story on the good we are doing and hoped that these "good news" stories would be aired during prime time instead of the usual "bad news" stories.

Civil Affairs teams had helped get the Rasafa Health Center a building for their clinic from one of Saddam's cousins, then remodeled and equipped it. The clinic dentist, a woman named Alyaa Ahmed Aziz, told me, "It is a free clinic for all with the primary mission of serving the 6,000 children in this district of Baghdad who are less than 5 years old." Here again we handed out beanie babies to the children. Sgt. Jared Shumate, a communications specialist with our command quipped, "This is definitely the best part of my day. How can you beat handing out toys to children?" I still found it a little surrealistic to be in a children's clinic, wearing a helmet, 45 pounds of body armor, magazine pouches with 210 rounds of ammo, and carrying a loaded rifle with a round in the chamber.

As we headed down Omar Bin Yassif Street to our next stop, I remembered MAJ Hassig had told us all during the convoy briefing this morning, "Do not point your weapon at anyone unless they are threatening you to the point that lethal force is necessary." "Instead," he said, "Look at people and wave at them. Then see if they wave back. You can tell a lot by their body language. Remember we are here to help the Iraqis, not to frighten them." This was good advice and I took it. Besides, the children almost always waved to us first!

Our third stop was a "deaf and mute" school that served 176 children and a workshop for adults. Here Civil Affairs projects included remodeling the building, repairing and donating a bus, and donating desks, computers, and replacing a $75,000 generator to provide the power supply. Zenia Mahadi, one of the woman supervisors told me, "We still need better security, higher salaries, and air-conditioning. Since they are paid about $60 per month, I don't blame her for asking. Today they were sewing orange jumpsuits for Ministry of Labor work crews under the spinning ceiling fans. I couldn't help but wonder if Al Zarqawi's terrorist group had put in an order for this color earlier in the year for their kidnapping victims.

We now headed east along the Tigris River, passing donkeys pulling carts piled with propane bottles, scores of grimy car repair lots, and rows of Chevy S-10 pickup trucks converted into tow-trucks waiting for their next call. We crossed Al Rasheed Street into the run-down Riyadh district of south-central Baghdad, splashing through puddles of green sewer slime as we turned down one narrow street after another. As I scanned the rooftops and the buildings, whenever I saw children, they would smile and wave to me and I would smile and wave back.

Finally we pulled around a fenced grassy park with trees and shelters surrounded by a low fence. I was told that this was the "Iron Broom" Park Project. Here the 1st Armored Division took a garbage dump and transformed it into a park last year. Now our 478th Civil Affairs team checks on it regularly and today we had beanie babies for the local children. Here more than anywhere, they came out of seemingly nowhere until in less than 15 or 20 minutes there must have been a hundred small children, some with parents, and some with older brothers or sisters, mobbing us for beanie babies. Unfortunately, we ran out of toys before children but we promised to come back soon.

Then off we went back to the west, all the way to the bend in the Tigris, past nice houses, residential areas, and finally date palm orchards with orange trees planted underneath, to the campus of Baghdad University. Here the university had donated a place to build a new gas station, with 4 gas pumps and 2 diesel pumps. The groundwork and paving was done and when the project is completed, believe it or not, this will be the first gas station built in the Karada district of Baghdad since 1967.

Next we drove east along Jamia Street to Kamal Junblat Square. We stopped nearby while a British officer with us scouted out a possible assistance project. MAJ Valdez in my vehicle saw a refreshment stand nearby and bought us all a can of soda pop. Meanwhile two boys came by and I gave them each a candy bar. Then we turned north and drove to the Al-Ziewa Neighborhood Clinic near the Babylon Hotel. CERP money was used here to build a second floor, and soon the clinic will receive $54,000 worth of medical equipment including defibrillators.

Our last stop of the day was on the south bank of the Tigris just downstream from the 14 July Bridge and across from the Green Zone. Here was the site that had been chosen for a new soccer field. A great project considering Iraq played their best Olympic soccer games in history this month. Then a man told us that he saw a dead body along the riverbank that had just floated downstream. After we reported the body to the Iraqi Police, we drove across the bridge back to the Green Zone. Tomorrow we will go out again to try and bring more life and less death to Baghdad.

Staff Sergeant Dave Conklin, 350th Civil Affairs Command, meets some new friends outside the Karada Youth Center that is scheduled to open in early September in a former residence of one of Saddam Hussein's relatives. The Command is sponsoring the project under the Commanders Emergency Relief Program (CERP). The center will serve over 5000 school-age children in south-central Baghdad. Wednesday Aug. 25, 2004. (P8250102) (Photo --Dave Conklin)

10. Getting Short

Baghdad, Iraq, 2350 Hours Charlie +1, Wednesday, 01Sep2004

Friends and relatives sometimes pass on my letters, and sometimes add their thoughts as well:

To: Bob Toll (E-mail); Geri Ransom (E-mail); Joanne Wainwright (E-mail); Lisa Parker (Home) (E-mail); Mo Sanders (E-mail 2)
Subject: FW: [Fwd: Last Wednesday in Baghdad]
This is from Susie's cousin - he rejoined the army about a year ago and volunteered to go to Iraq. He is insane.
--Susie S

AND

Dave

Your reports are fascinating--and it IS wonderful to hear some good news about what you guys are doing over there. The kids look so cute and open. Hope that their country is a bit more settled before they are adults! Pennsylvania is so bucolic, it's hard to imagine your life over there, and the many, many people who are struggling to make Iraq work as a country. There were some interviews with some of the drivers from other countries on the radio. They sounded as if they were thrilled to have jobs. They may not want the hostilities to end too soon. Where do the Iraqis get their food? Are they able to find fresh fruits and vegetables? Have you been able to try Iraqi food there? Be careful!
JoAnn

Hi JoAnn:

Thanks for writing. It's always great to hear from you, and to remember what "normal" is. Sorry to hear about your mother. I am hoping for the best. My father just had his 91st birthday and I pray that I can come home and still find him in good health. As for your question, Iraqi food is a lot like Turkish and Balkan food! The shops look the same and the goats and sheep are hung in the windows without refrigeration. There is a lot of irrigated cropland all up and down the Tigris and Euphrates. In the winter, oranges, limes, and lemons are popular. In the early summer the Iraqis bring me apricots. Watermelons and cantaloupes are popular during the summer as are tomatoes and cucumbers. Since the middle of August the pomegranates and dates have been ripening. I picked a branch of dates in a nearby neighborhood today and brought it back for others to try. The date palms grow like weeds here!

Also in the southern marshes there is rice and fish and the Iraqis make a great dish of rice, almonds and olives, with a fish filet on top. In the two or three cafes in the Green Zone we can get Iraqi food--including chicken, shish kebabs, and shishche or sausages. But the KBR dining facilities here have the same standard fare (safe, but boring) of meat, mashed potatoes, canned vegetables, frozen cake, canned pop, and milk or juice in little boxes. Keep in touch JoAnn.
Dave

Baghdad, Iraq, 1020 Hours Charlie +1, Thursday, 02Sep2004

I was in a festive mood today for two reasons. First, it was "TGIT" day (thank God it's Thursday). We are allowed to sleep a little longer on Friday morning and we are allowed time to write letters and wash clothes. But having Friday as a "holy day" instead of having a "weekend" really screws up my week. Actually the Arabic word for Friday *yowm al-Jum'a* means "meeting day" and Saturday *yowm al-sebat* means "Sabbath day." I am always looking at the calendar to figure out what day it is since the week and the work seem to be never ending.

The second reason for happiness today is that Major Mike Dunne, a reservist from Buffalo, New York and my boss in the G8 shop at the 350th HQ announced that our unit will have a change of command ceremony on October 4th with the 353rd CACOM from New York, and we should start preparing for redeployment back to the states. He introduced me to his replacement Major Furman Oxendine who is here with the advance party. Most of their troops will arrive after September 20th.

Things will start happening fast now. I still have a basket full of contracts to bid out, to write, track deliveries, and make payments on. I have four news releases to research, write, and market by the 15th and another media escort beginning the 20th. But I also need to ask around about what I options I have for retiring or continuing in the Army Reserve and even check on job opportunities with some of these international companies that are here if the money is there. I also want to fill in the blanks on my journal and start researching a new book in the evenings.

Now we will also begin out-processing, equipment and office turnover, and training our replacements when they arrive. This week we turn in our "Jaylist" (JLST) chemical suits and atropine nerve agent antidote injectors and have an "in-ranks" inspection of personal equipment. On September 10th we will listen to briefings in the evening and fill out checklists and statements. Next week we go on our own to the palace clinic to use a palm pilot to fill out a medical screening questionnaire, then go to the post office to mail anything else we don't need that won't fit in our duffle bags.

On September 30th we will have a customs check and load our footlockers into ISU-90 Conex boxes to be shipped to Balad Air Base for transport back to Fort Bragg. We will follow sometime after October 4th via Kuwait, where we will turn in our body armor. So now I have something definite to look forward to besides my never-ending "donut of misery" computerized tour of duty countdown that someone passed on to me. By the way it tells me my tour of duty is now 92 percent done and I have only 507 hours and 57 minutes to go, but who's counting?

SSG Dave Conklin points to some of the more than 1,000 signatures and comments in dozens of languages on the wall of the U.S. Embassy Badging Office building inside the front gate of the Presidential Palace Saturday, Sep. 11, 2004. (P9110010) (Photo --Dave Conklin)

Sometimes I get letters from people I don't even know:

Hi,
You don't know me but I work with [your sister] Rita at M&T Mortgage in Bellevue, Washington. Rita has been sending me your e-mails over the past months. I have enjoyed learning what's really

going on there--testimonials unfiltered by today's biased media. I wanted to take this chance to congratulate you on being able to come home. I also wanted to personally thank you and your colleagues for your commitment to making our home safer and that part of the world better for all those people--people who suffered for so long under a despicable regime.

    I would also like to apologize on the behalf of the many Americans who don't appreciate what you're doing. The vast majority only hear how many got killed today, not the good all of you are doing. I also apologize for those who have disrespected your Commander in Chief. Everyone's entitled to their opinion but many go too far. I don't want to take more of your time, so once again, congratulations, and I wish you a safe trip home
Sincerely,
Tim Lucas

Baghdad, Iraq, 2321 Hours Charlie +1, Saturday, 04Sep2004

I write another letter to my wife:

> Mary,
> Great talking to you on the phone tonight sweetie! And Dacia and Randy too! My lunch trip with MAJ Oxendine, the new G8 and SGT DaCosta to the Al Rasheed Hotel today was interrupted by a mortar shell that landed in the tree island near the front door. The good news is that it missed us by about two minutes. The bad news was that the air conditioning has been broken for three days and the food has been bad. I remember saying I would die for a good steak, but I would hate to be killed on the way to eat BAD food! The temperature today was 114 F, but came down to about 102 F by 7:30 p.m. By the way I decided to go to the palace dining room for dinner tonight. It hasn't been bombed in more than a week!
> Very funny picture you sent! By the way I forgot to tell you that I got your "mutual orgasm" card—Are you sure this is our insurance company? The other day I also got the "butterfly" card! YES IT BUZZED AWAY RIGHT IN FRONT OF ME. You know me; I then had to try it on someone else. So I picked the new Air Force girl that I thought might be a screamer--yep! She screamed so loud it scared everyone around her! Then, of course, the rest of the guys got it and basically no one was spared who came into the office the

whole day—soldiers, Juliet the cleaning lady, interpreters—we even put the thing in a contract file folder and scared the commander half to death!
Thanks for an entertaining day last Thursday!
Love, Dave

SSG Dave Conklin, alias "Sheik Abu Daoud Al-Mustafa" tries on an Iraqi himmel at the Baghdad Contracting Office with interpreters Suhad, Nibras, and Dr. Moyaad Razook Sunday, Aug. 8, 2004. (Dave8) (Photo --Dave Conklin)

Republican Guard Compound, Green Zone, 2045 Hours Charlie +1, Thursday, 09Sep2004

It was warm and clear tonight. Heck it's warm and clear every night here in Baghdad. But tonight our office staff of ten was invited to the monthly party at the Triple Canopy House. Triple Canopy Protective Services is a private company based in Chicago that provides personal security escorts for Iraqi ministers and other civilian organizations.

They are located in a large walled house and yard in the Republican Guard Compound on the edge of the Green Zone. This area is strictly off limits to those who don't live here and we had to wait at the gate for an escort through the compound, past the large helo pad with two Sikorsky helicopters, to the end of the road where I parked the bus. Uday Hussein had this row of ten houses built for Ministry of Defense Generals and their families. The layout of each of the large flat-roofed three-story houses with large rooms and kitchens, open courtyards, second-story driveways, walled compounds and swimming pools is identical. But this particular house was Uday's, and Uday's house had some special features added such as two-inch thick bulletproof glass and doors that lock from the outside. Speculation is that without these locks, the girls he picked up would not have stayed quite as long as they did.

We brought some soda pop and the Triple Canopy folks provided the food and mixed the drinks. They even had a cooler full of Corona beer and a bowl of sliced limes. Most of us wore our shorts or swimsuits so we could take a dip in Uday's pool. The rectangular pool had a shallow 1.3-meter end and deep 3-meter end and was large enough for the ten of us plus more. Like most pools here in the Green Zone it was paved with blue tile, even the bottom. This made the drop-off from the shallow to the deep end very slippery. This pool was not for non-swimmers.

The folks who live and work out of Uday's house these days are not keen on giving out much information, especially their names. But over a few Bacardi and cokes I did meet some of the crew such as Hal the bartender, "OD" who just got back from the Philippines where he plopped down cash to buy a vacation condominium, and "AK" their pony-tailed armorer who spent most of his time in the arms room. AK showed me a number of rifles they had collected, including an 1870's Turkish lever action breechloader, and a couple of nickel-plated AK-47s that he guessed were used only by honor guards in parades or given out by Saddam or Uday as gifts to friends. Having a nickel-plated AK-47 on your wall was a signal not to mess with you because you knew "The Man."

I spoke to one of the Titan employees who worked in the golden domed gate near the old Ministry of Information building. She was in Afghanistan as a Civil Affairs specialist before joining Titan to test local hires for their English language skills. She said she is still in the Army Reserve and drills once a month with a unit here in Iraq. I asked if she thought the next attack on the Green Zone might take place this weekend during the Imam's birthday and the third anniversary of September 11th. She agreed that Saturday or Sunday would be a prime time for attacks by Abu Musab Al Zarqawi's terrorists.

A nickel plated AK-47 hangs on the wall in the den of the former house of Uday Hussein in the Republican Guard Compound. Uday may have had them made for honor guards, parades, and to give as gifts. Thursday, Sept. 9, 2004. (P9090038) (Photo --Dave Conklin)

Haifa Street, Baghdad, Iraq, 0625 Hours Charlie +1, Sunday, 12Sep2004

For the second day in a row I didn't need an alarm to wake me up. This time my windows rattled and the whole building shook from not one, but a whole salvo of mortars landing nearby. Dawn was breaking as I hopped out of bed and pulled on my DCU trousers and boots. When I opened the curtains I could see thick, black smoke rising from the south wing of the palace, about one-quarter mile south. I had my M16 in my room but of course ran down the stairs to the office to get my camera. I found my Air Force and Navy colleagues already there. They were halfway to the palace gym when the mortars hit and ran all the way back. I grabbed my camera and then headed for the roof of the building. When I got there more mortars were striking—to the east now, then to the north, then the west.

I watched as fire broke out a mile west near the Tomb of the Unknown Soldier when a mortar made a direct hit through the bed of a civilian transport truck parked on the street and scattered twisted metal from its sidewalls onto the dry grass. Then at about 6:50 a.m. I heard a boom and saw a cloud of smoke behind the old Ministry of Information building to the north. Now the sounds of heavy machine gun fire from the same location, then Kiowa and Apache attack helicopters joined the show. Finally I heard another loud boom and followed a large cloud of black smoke which I assumed was a vehicle fire.

The mortars stopped after more than a dozen had landed in the Green Zone. I went back inside, finished dressing, and turned on BBC radio in my room. By 7:20 a.m. there was already a report on the attack. I went downstairs to the office and turned on my cell phone. Soon I got a call from MAJ Dunne at the 350th HQ. He asked how we were and I said fine, and asked him the same question. He said they had some damage but couldn't talk in the clear. I met him later at the Al Rasheed Hotel and he said that one of the mortars hit the Korean Embassy building 50 yards from the 350th HQ building, killing one and injuring two local workers there. For the first time, the workers had decided to stay there overnight so they could get the work done sooner. It cost them dearly.

I told everyone that this would be a good day to wear body armor if they were going outside. I had expected this attack yesterday on September 11th, but maybe I had my calendar off by a day. Today I planned to mail some packages but decided to wait until lunchtime. I hoped that the Steel Dragon chow hall, near Haifa Street where I heard the machine guns this morning, would be open. It was. I mailed my packages at the postal section nearby then went in and got a plate of fried fish, noodles and gravy, grapes, and ice tea. I found a table and put my M16 on the floor under the table, then took off my Kevlar helmet and body armor and stacked it along the wall with everyone else's.

I sat across from SGT Gregory with the 1-9 Cavalry. He said he was hungry since the chow hall was closed for breakfast. I asked if he knew what the black smoke in this direction was from this morning. He said that his unit went out on patrol on Haifa Street to find out where the mortars were coming from when a suicide bomber ran his car into one of our Bradley fighting vehicles and blew himself up. Our GIs evacuated amid grenades and small arms fire with only two injured and a crowd gathered around and on top of the Bradley, waving their AK-47s and the flag of Abu Musab Al Zarqawi's militia.

I guess we still had a few tricks too, because the soldiers called for air support and a helicopter fired a rocket at the Bradley, blowing it up and killing the attackers. I later heard that some journalists said that "civilians" and "children" were killed. These "civilians" were armed terrorists, and I know that they give rifles and hand grenades to boys as young as 9 years old and teach them how to kill us. Later we found out that attacks had been made all over Baghdad, at Camp Victory and on the road to BIAP. There a suicide car bomber blew up three Humvees injuring three of our troops in a convoy. I heard there was a total of seven car bombs in Iraq today.

I was busy with office work during the afternoon, but at about 6 p.m. I put on my body armor to drive to dinner and on the way took some photos of the Korean Embassy building and supply truck that had been hit by mortars. I wanted to be back inside by dark in case they started firing more salvos this evening. Sure enough as I finish writing this at 8:30 p.m. they started hammering us with mortars again.

Today's attack was the most intense mortar and rocket barrages on the Green Zone in the nine months that I have been here so far. By the end of the day I heard that at least 37 people were killed and over 100 wounded here in Baghdad.

Staff Sergeant Dave Conklin, 350th Civil Affairs Command, looks from the roof of the Finance building in the Green Zone early Sunday morning, at a column of smoke rising from a mortar strike near the south wing of the Presidential Palace during the most intense mortar and rocket barrages ever seen in central Baghdad September 12, 2004. (DSCF200456) (Photo -- SSG Todd Babin)

350th Civil Affairs Command HQ, Riverside Compound, Green Zone, 0844 Hours Charlie +1, Monday, 13Sep2004

I could sense that something was wrong. SGT Tina Beller, our public affairs specialist, was not her usual talkative self during our staff meeting so I waited until everyone had left and asked if she was OK. She finally opened up, "I didn't sleep much at all last night because I kept seeing their faces," she said. "Whose faces?" I asked. "The men who were in the Korean Embassy building when the rocket hit yesterday morning. I was coming back from the palace at 6:30 a.m. when I heard a loud explosion.

"I saw a Gurkha guard in the middle of the street waving his hands over his head as a distress signal so I went to see what was wrong." Tina went on, "When I got there it had just happened. I'm used to seeing blood, but not a man with his brains blown out, or a man walking aimlessly bleeding from what used to be his jaw. A Navy SEAL was the first one there and was treating the other one when I came. I tried to ask the wounded man if there was anyone else inside, but he didn't answer me. Only later I realized that the two who had lived were probably deafened by the blast as well as injured. By now SGT Perkins was there, and the SEAL asked me to go call an ambulance. Then someone told me to go wash up and get the blood off of my clothes. I hadn't even noticed that my arm was covered with this man's blood" (Carroll, 2006, pp. 261-265).

"It finally got to me when I was taking a shower," she said. "I found myself scrubbing my arms and knees over and over again. When I came out of my trance, I just sat there in the shower and cried for I don't know how long. Last night I kept seeing their faces. I felt so guilty that I was there but couldn't save them. Nobody I've talked to so far understands what I feel like. Only one man who was in Vietnam understood." She said. "I understand," I said, as I mentioned replaying in my head the ambush I went through last April and feeling the same way for a few days. This evening I talked to SGT Will Perkins who was also there. He said he hadn't got much sleep since then either.

One Iraqi worker was killed and two injured when a 127mm rocket hit the corner of a former residence in the Riverside Compound in the Green Zone being remodeled as the Korean Embassy early Sunday morning, September 12, 2004. (P912020044) (Photo --Dave Conklin)

Afterwards I received messages from some of my combat veteran friends who knew exactly what we had experienced:

Dave,
   I understand also. When talking to Tina please try to let her know that all loss of life is a waste but her trying to help was the right response even if she doesn't think it saved anyone it does show that she is still the same person she was before she went there. The horror of wartime casualties never quite leaves you but the fact that you tried like hell to help means your humanity is still intact.
Pete

Tina's reaction is not uncommon, and perhaps more to be expected from a woman than a man since women are nurturing creatures by nature to a greater degree than men. But we men often experience the same "I failed" reaction as I did the first time I couldn't "help" a fatally wounded soldier and every time thereafter, but to lesser degrees as I became more mentally hardened to battle and casualties.

What Tina needs is someone to talk with about her experience, and while almost anyone can listen, someone with "counseling" training is far better than someone without. Your correspondent (his name escapes me although I know you've told me) should encourage her to seek out a chaplain or a medical person with such training. If he tries that and she doesn't follow his advice, he ought to find such a person, explain the situation, and let the counselor make an unsolicited visit. Tina will work her way thru this but she'll do it faster and with less pain if she gets help with the process.

Please feel free to pass my thoughts to your friend.
Frank Scott Johnson (COL, IN, Ret.)

Dave,

It doesn't sound pretty over there. Can't even imagine what you all are seeing, doing and putting up with. One wonders if you'll ever sleep well again. We're beginning to see lots of stories of local boys who didn't come home, or who've come back terribly wounded. And then to think of all the Iraqis who have suffered and will suffer for so long to come--so very sad. Just wish I could believe that all will not have been in vain. The news has been so very bad lately, I'm afraid to check the e-mail for the news. It seems a bit silly to say, "Be careful," but do!
Joanne

Bozeman, Montana, 1648 Hours Tango +1, Wednesday, 22Sep2004

A letter from my daughter:

Hey Dad:
Congratulations on receiving the Bronze Star. Mom said you would not tell her how you got it. Well, whatever you did you

deserve it. I hope you are doing well and staying out of trouble. Take care and we all love and miss you over here in Bozeman. See you soon.
Love ya.
Dacia English

Hi Dacia:
You always were so nosy! But I guess you are right. In my usual style I didn't give your dear mother much information, but then like some people who get awards, I was still trying to ask myself "why me?" when there are many others who deserve more. I didn't do any one thing to deserve this. Basically it was just to recognize my 16 hour-per-day work for 9 months trying to support as many missions as I could and keep the people around me alive and well at the same time. What I am most proud of is that I didn't have to kill anyone to get a medal. It was for helping people--both Americans and Iraqis. I hope that explains it for you.
Love,
Dad

Unknown Soldier Monument, Baghdad, 1948 Hours Charlie +1, Thursday, 23Sep2004

"Quif! Quif! (Stop! Stop!) yelled the Iraqi security guard as he raised his AK-47 and pointed it toward the figure dressed in a white *dishdasha* and black *kughtra* headdress running in the evening twilight. But Major Greg Vialle, also known by his Baghdad Hash House Harriers name as "Pocket Spy" did not hear or see the guard behind him. Lucky for him, his co-hare, Marla, who spoke some Arabic, was far enough behind to see what was going down. She called to the guard, who asked why he was dressed that way and running? She replied in Arabic, "It's like a game." Game hell—this was turning out to be another "combat hash."

Today was supposed to be my day off so I could start packing for redeployment, but it didn't turn out that way. The end of the fiscal year was upon us. In the morning I had to get over to the 350th HQ to download files from the Army financial system and finish scrubbing our ledgers and document registers and finish obligating our $14 million budget for Operations, Overseas Humanitarian Disaster and Civil Assistance, and the Commander's Emergency Response Program. At the same time, LTG Casey and a couple of his deputies stopped by to look at our HQ for new office space.

I had lunch at the Presidential Palace so I could attend the briefing we were preparing for a visit from MG Buzz Altshuler, the CAPOC commander at Fort Bragg. Then back to the 350th HQ to take photos of a promotion and award ceremony. Finally I headed back to the Contracting Office to welcome my third incoming commander in nine months, Air Force Captain Louis Orndorff, a native of Boise, Idaho who is deployed for four months from Ramstein Air Base in Germany. I skipped the dinner hour and at 5:30 p.m. headed over to the palace parking lot to become "Al Zheimer" again and run with the "hashemites" to loosen up and get my hour-long run in for the week. It was still about 95 F when we started running, but I desperately needed the exercise and mental release, and this might be the last hash for me before I leave Baghdad.

Tonight was the *"dishdasha dash"* hash run and Pocket Spy was the hare—the first one out to lay the trail. As usual the local Iraqi population in the Green Zone loved to see so many people dressed in their traditional Arab clothing, and they waved and greeted us as we ran through the neighborhoods and thoroughfares in our dishdashas. Of course they were always asking what we were chasing. From as little as 6 to 10 of us last February, there are now over forty regular hashers. I always say there is safety in numbers, and I'm staying close together and yelling something in English so I don't end up like Pocket Spy.

Letters from Baghdad   151

The Free Baghdad Hash House Harriers (with Al Zheimer kneeling on the right) pose for the camera in the CPA parking lot before the first "Dishdasha Dash" Friday, Mar 5, 2004. (IMG_0431)(Photo -- Will Merrill)

11. Return to Kuwait

350th Civil Affairs Command HQ, Riverside Compound, Green Zone, 1036 Hours Charlie, Monday, 04Oct2004

For the last group of 50 of us remaining in Baghdad our war was officially over. The Transfer of Authority or "TOA" ceremony went off without a hitch thanks to several days of practice for all of us. Now our colors were cased, the 353rd CACOM's colors were uncased, and Deputy C3 (Operations) Marine MG Meyer and incoming BG Hashim both gave short talks to those of us in the rank and file who were part of the ceremony.

The day had not been without trouble though. While I was saying goodbye to Melad Al Jaburi, my Arabic teacher for the past eight months, the windows in the cabin rattled from a car bomb explosion. I found out later that Checkpoint 12, the one we will use to go to the airport today, was targeted and a soldier was killed. At 9:00 a.m. I climbed up to the third floor of the 350th HQ in the Palace of the King of Jordan to finish my last lesson to my replacement, SFC Diane Medina from Brooklyn, New York.

While we were talking, a loud "ka-BOOM" split the air and shook the whole building. I waited a few seconds for a second boom, then hearing none, raced to the window with Medina right behind me. Directly across the Tigris River on the other side of the Palestine Hotel a dirty grey cloud was rising. Soon the rising smoke turned black and grew in intensity. There was no question in my mind that I was looking at the latest car bomb explosion. I heard later that a suicide bomber had run into an SUV convoy, killing a number of women and children who were nearby, as well as six or seven Westerners.

I unconsciously began describing that this must be a car bomb and the grey smoke was from the explosion, then the black smoke would be from the vehicles, upholstery, fuel tanks and bodies burning. Then I caught myself and realized that this was not helping SFC Medina cope with the realities of her first two weeks in a war zone.

After the ceremony I had just enough time to go back to the Contracting Office, load my duffle bag and rucksack, and say farewell to all my friends, both American and Iraqi, including CPT Louis Orndorff, CPT Kevin Finch, Finance 1LT Gary Drosdowski, MSG's Lewis, Cunningham, and Cacho, SSG's Jimenez, Deroy-Spell, Hamilton, and Todd Babin, SGT Greg Nelson, our secretaries Nibras and Raghad, and our Iraqi grounds and gatekeepers.

Then I took my last drive in our Nissan Pathfinder to the 350th HQ to load into the two buses waiting to take us to the airport. We left at 2 p.m. with a 3-Humvee escort. These buses were not armored, and we traveled in Kevlar and body armor with our M16s loaded just in case. Since our airplane did not show up, we stopped instead at Camp Victory's Tent City and spent the night in tent number 99, cooled by a fan at either end. The night was warm and clear as usual, and thankfully quiet.

We held an impromptu award ceremony in the dark for MAJ Eversman who saved COL Lyke's life during a convoy last April, but that's another story. My boss MAJ Dunne and I smoked the last of our Cuban cigars before turning in for the night while a small group was playing poker under the camouflage net behind the tent. This would be our last night in Iraq.

A group of soldiers from the 350th Civil Affairs Command play poker while waiting for a C-130 cargo plane flight out of Iraq on a warm clear night under a camouflage net in "tent city" at South Camp Victory, near the Baghdad International Airport, Oct. 4, 2004. (DCP02684) (Photo --Dave Conklin)

Tent City, Camp Victory, Iraq, 0430 Hours Charlie, Tuesday, 05Oct2004

It was still dark when SGM James Maree yelled, "Get up! Get up! Tent 99." Others began re-packing their duffle bags. I headed for the last known porta-potty I saw yesterday. After packing, at 5 a.m. we loaded our duffle and rucksacks onto a cargo truck and kept only our Kevlar, body armor, rifle, and carry-on bag. At 5:30 a.m. the new "Coalition Café" dining hall, just across the gravel parking area east of tent city, opened for breakfast and we were already in line. By 6 a.m. when we boarded the buses again for the short ride to the BIAP air terminal, it was no longer dark.

We were told our flight "Crone 45" (or was it "Glide 45?") would leave at zero-eight-thirty hours sharp and to be at the terminal to palletize our duffle at least three hours early. We arrived only two hours early but had our two pallets built less than 30 minutes later. "Crone 45" finally touched down at 10:00 a.m. All 50 of us clambered on board through the side door, had our earplugs in, and were strapped down by 10:30 a.m. But the plane spends the next hour sitting on the tarmac—with us in cramped nylon seats, backpacks on our laps and rifles by our sides in the sweltering heat in full "battle rattle." The mood improves when COL David Cunningham takes an American flag out of his backpack and hangs it over our baggage pallets to be with us as we fly out of Iraq.

Finally at 11:20 a.m. we felt the lumbering C-130 start to move and before we knew it we were airborne as the pilot began his combat takeoff procedures making a hard left turn, then up, then down. The next sensation was the sound of loud metallic "punk-punk," "punk-punk" noises from the rear of the plane as the pilot fired "chaff" flares to deflect any heat-seeking ground to air missiles that might be aimed in our direction. As we gained altitude, the air cooled inside and the sweat ceased dripping from our foreheads. I took off my Kevlar helmet and opened the front of my body armor vest for some ventilation. For the next two hours we sat motionless as the plane flew south. I used the opportunity to take a nap as did SGT Higgenbotham and MAJ Jeff Jurasik across from me. SFC Diaz, on my left, was snacking on some tortilla chips he dug out of his backpack. On my right, MAJ Mike Dunne was reading a novel.

I could see sand through the small porthole above and to the left of me as we circled to land at Ali al-Salem Air Base in Kuwait. It was 12:30 p.m. when we landed (Kuwait and Iraq were for now on the same time since Iraq had gone to standard time a month earlier than Kuwait). The pallets were taken off the plane by a forklift that brought them to our bus where we all pitched in to transfer our duffle bags and rucksacks to a truck that would follow our bus to Camp Doha near Kuwait City.

As we got off the bus at Camp Doha, I guessed that the temperature was about 110 F, thankfully about 10 or 15 degrees cooler than it was when I was here in July. We were taken to warehouse building #18, Bay #132 full of bunk beds and lockers where we would be staying, both men and women, until we moved out again. As we unloaded, we were greeted by those from our unit who left on earlier flights as well as those from our Jordan HAC (Humanitarian Assistance Center) and Kuwait HOC that we hadn't seen for months. After locking up our weapons, we were free to shop at the PX, go to the Marble Palace pool, eat at the food court or dining hall, check our e-mail at the post library, or go to tonight's movie (Bourne

Supremacy) which I did. It was great to have some free time and a few places to go. But like most of us, I still ducked each time I heard a loud noise or a slamming door.

Terminal at Ali al-Salem Air Base in Kuwait. Oct. 6, 2004. (DCP02690) (Photo --Dave Conklin)

Bldg. 18, Bay 132, Camp Doha, Kuwait, 0900 Hours Bravo +1, Wednesday, 06Oct2004

We were given the day off, but still had to be present for the daily 0900 hours and 1945 hours formations for accountability and information. This morning we learned that our flight to Fort Bragg would leave at 0200 hours on Saturday morning. So back planning from that we were told that customs and packing would take up most of Friday, driving our 120 Humvees to the seaport would be done on Thursday, and today all we had to do was clean our weapons.

So I and several others spent the next hour disassembling and thoroughly cleaning our M16 rifles and M9 Beretta pistols on a picnic table outside our bay before going to lunch. The wall-mounted TVs in the dining facility were always tuned to Fox News or CNN. As we ate lunch the news announced that an IED (Improvised Explosive Device) had been found in the Green Zone Café yesterday and successfully defused. After lunch I walked to the library to sign up to use an internet computer to check my e-mail. Once inside I heard someone call my name. It was Clark from the Montana National Guard headquarters in Helena. His CERT Team (Computer Emergency Response Team) had been deployed here in June. I promised to stop in and see them in Building 10 before I left.

As I walked the streets of Camp Doha, browsed the shops in the Food Court and the PX, and ate at the dining facility, I couldn't help but notice that virtually all of the vendors, workers, food service people and even trash collectors were dark-skinned Indians and Pakistanis. I don't think I ever saw a Kuwaiti outside of his BMW or Chevy Suburban.

The temperature in Kuwait averaged about 10 to 15 degrees warmer than in Baghdad but it had cooled to a balmy 109 F today. Nevertheless, cold water here was as rare as hen's teeth. We had boxes of bottled water on pallets outside the building and a refrigerator in our bay. We would bring in a box or two and stock the refrigerator with a warm bottle as we took out a cool one (the bottles never were inside long enough to get cold). Even in the shower you only needed to turn on the cold water faucet to get hot water. But the strangest thing I experienced was the steam bath my rear end got every time I flushed the toilet!

Highway sign on route 40 in Kuwait. Oct. 6, 2004. (DCP02720) (Photo --Dave Conklin)

Bldg. 18, Bay 132, Camp Doha, Kuwait, 0500 Hours Bravo +1, Thursday, 07Oct2004

As I climbed out of my top bunk to get dressed, I wondered why I volunteered to take SGT DaCosta's place on the 80-person Humvee detail today when I could have taken the day off. No matter, I planned to take my cameras and take pictures of the desert and all the camels I could find during the day. We were told to have breakfast, shower and get our weapons for a 6:00 a.m. formation before boarding buses to go to the vehicle marshalling yard where we would link up with 120 Humvees that were freighted from Baghdad last month. These were un-armored

Humvees without doors or tops that would be loaded on a ship next week by four of our soldiers who would stay to do that so the vehicles could be sent back to our units in the states. Our job was to drive them in three convoys of 40 each from Camp Doha to the SPOD (Sea Port of Debarkation) about 30 miles south of here and 20 miles south of Kuwait City.

Hurry up and wait became the watchword of the day. We arrived at the marshalling yard on North Camp Doha at 6:30 a.m., paired off and got in to the first 40 Humvees, started them up and drove them to the gate—where we waited for two and a half hours for our Kuwaiti Police escort. We reached the SPOD by 11:00 a.m. by driving on the seventh ring freeway, then a convoy route through a Kuwait Oil Company town. Then we waited an hour at the gate while another convoy of 5-ton trucks was checked in. Each of our vehicles had to be checked in by the Navy LCDR in charge or the civilian workers who used a bar code reader to read the labels glued on to the hood of each vehicle. Some vehicles even had RFID (Radio Frequency Identification) tag boxes wired to their fenders so they could be tracked by satellite imagery.

They let us stop only long enough to use the porta-potties and grab a bottle of water. Then the buses that followed us took us back for the next 40 Humvees. By the time we got back, we needed replacements for several heat casualties. We were not given any food or MREs so I was glad I had brought a couple of candy bars. We jumped in our next 40 vehicles, waited for our escort, and repeated the whole process. This time our Air Force escort vehicle got lost and led our bus through downtown Kuwait City on the way back to Camp Doha. We returned for the last group of Humvees at 5:30 p.m. Still no MREs or a break for chow.

The vehicle I received this time had a low tire so I had to drive over to the service bay across the street and borrow an air hose before I got back in line. The sun had gone down by the time we left and it was dark as we drove down the seventh ring highway. Despite the fact that this was the third trip, our Air Force escort car missed the highway exit and we were on our way to Saudi Arabia. There was nothing we could do but follow until he realized his mistake and turned around. When he missed the turn off to the SPOD entrance, I refused to follow and just stopped on the road until he turned around and came back. After the last vehicles were checked in and parked at 8:00 p.m., we were allowed to eat at the local dining facility just before it closed. It was 10:30 p.m. before we got back to our bunks. An eight-hour day was doubled into a sixteen-hour day with heat casualties by poor planning and bad leadership. By the way, I didn't see a single camel to photograph all day.

Our 120 HMMWVs ready for the trip to the port. Oct. 7, 2004. (DCP02706) (Photo -- Dave Conklin)

Bldg. 18, Bay 132, Camp Doha, Kuwait, 0745 Hours Bravo +1, Friday, 08Oct2004

I salute COL Mel Howry, our JAG officer, as I pass him on the way to breakfast. I am ready to leave this place. It is a sprawling camp of giant warehouses sandwiched between the shallow shore of the Persian Gulf to the east and a massive oil-fired electrical generating plant just to the west. Each warehouse has dozens of interior bays that have been remodeled into everything from barracks to bathrooms, dining halls to offices. The temperature is already 85F outside and it would be a bright sunny day except for the always present low hanging smog from the constant plumes of smoke that pour out of the four power plant smokestacks. I have been here only three days and already I have a runny nose and sniffles from the ever-present air pollution.

As I walk down the street I see Indian workers loading concrete barriers onto flatbed trucks. One of our officers tells me that Camp Doha has been leased from the Kuwaiti government since the Gulf War but the lease is up this year and everything will be relocated to Camp Arifjan, south of Kuwait City.

After breakfast we get ready for the Air Force customs airmen by putting our mattresses on the floor and dumping all the contents of our duffle bag and rucksack onto them. One airman rifles through all of my gear, watches as I repack, then helps me put the bags onto the baggage truck waiting outside. Afterwards I head over to Building 10 to find the Montana Guard soldiers and say hello. Major Stephan, Chief Warrant Officer, Art Pembroke and I have lunch together and talk about who we know is deployed where and for how long. Art tells me they will be in Kuwait until at least next April. I wish them well and head for the library before dinner and "lockdown" at 6:00 p.m. At that time we will get our out-briefs, customs checks on our carry-on bags, and load the buses for the trip to the airport at 10:30 p.m.

Network Ops Center at Camp Doha, Kuwait. From left: MAJ Stephan, SSG Dave Conklin, CWO Pembroke. Oct. 8, 2004. (DCP02733) (Photo --Dave Conklin)

Over Shannon, Ireland, 0720 Hours Zulu +1, Saturday, 09Oct2004

The sun was just coming over the horizon as our Boeing 757-200 ATA Airlines charter flight came in for a landing over the lush green rolling farm fields and rock fences of Shannon, Ireland. After nearly a year of sand and concrete, it is a real treat to see a whole country that looks like a golf course. While the plane is being refueled, we find our way to the airport bar where a long line of soldiers forms to buy the first pint of Guinness draft beer they've had in months, made even better by drinking it in the country where it comes from. Here I receive my first thank you's from an American couple here on vacation.

Our next refueling stop is Bangor, Maine, at 10:20 a.m. local time. I am able to call my wife from Bangor thanks to a group of veterans who operate a wonderful reception facility at the airport. To our surprise, both veterans, wives, and young people greet us with handshakes, hugs, banners, and even cell phones so we can call home.

As we fly south to Fort Bragg, I see the strangest sight I'm sure I will ever see on a commercial airliner. Hundreds of assault rifles and automatic pistols are laying everywhere. We take our weapons off of the floor and out of the overhead compartments and pass them back and forth as cleaning kits come out and we put the final touches on our cleaning jobs. As our plane touches down on U.S. soil at Pope Air Force Base, a cheer rings out and all hands are clapping. As we roll up to the Green Ramp, through the windows I can see a crowd waving banners and flags. Soon we are walking down the steps and shaking hands with the general and sergeant major of the Special Forces, Civil Affairs and Psychological Operations Command (CAPOC). It has been eighteen and a half hours since we left Kuwait.

Sergeant Geiger (left) has his first alcoholic beverage in 9 months at the airport bar in Shannon, Ireland. Oct. 9, 2004. (DCP02744) (Photo --Dave Conklin)

Old Division Area, Fort Bragg, 1216 Hours Romeo +1, Monday, 11Oct2004

Today I decided to read my e-mail and clean up my in-box on my computer. I saw that I had replies to the e-mail goodbye message I sent the Iraqi contractors below:

From: dave.conklin@us.army.mil
Subject: Shokran wa ma a salama! (Thanks and goodbye)
Date: Mon, 04 Oct 2004 12:16:25 -0400

>TO ALL:
>I am leaving the Baghdad Contracting Office and redeploying back to the U.S. with my unit. It's been great working with you all while I was at Baghdad Contracting and learning about Iraq, business in Iraq, and the wonderful Iraqi people. You are all great business professionals who taught me more than you may realize, including a bit of the Arabic language. I hope that I can return to Baghdad someday, and that when I do you will all be doing well, and the country of Iraq will be doing well.
>Thank you for everything.
>
>SSG Dave Conklin, USAR
>350th Civil Affairs Command

I was pleased to see that many of the Iraqi contractors I dealt with during the past year recognized my work and some sent e-mail replies:

safaya3@hotmail.com

Dear Alsalam aleykoom,
That is namely in Arabic (Peace upon you). You are the best person we have met him in all our work and we are very Prideful in that. We hope for you happy time with your family and we ask God to bless you and your family.
Best Regards
Bariq Co.

AND:

Dear Sir;
It has been my deep pleasure working with you in performing some contracts. I hope that to return home safely. And it has been said two things: 1-He who drinks Tigris water, should come back again one day; and, 2-the world is small, i.e. we may meet each other one day again...who knows. Thank you sir again...and thanks for working with you.
Haqqi Ismail Abid
For /Al-Wethiba General Contracting Bureau

AND:

najah jabbar <alraheem@hotmail.com>

Thank you Sir very much. I like to work with you because you are great man, and I am sorry for you leaving Iraq and i hope to back again and I hope the Iraq will be quiet in order to come many American peaple to visit my countery.
Thanks.

I had hoped that during my time in Iraq I would protect my soldiers, do no harm in helping the Iraqi's rebuild their country, and hopefully do a little bit of good whenever I could. If I did, that would be mission success for me.

Part 2. 2005 - My War as a Defense Contractor

12. Return to Iraq

The tongue of the people is a book on the floor.
– Translated Inscription above Presidential Palace Door

The Walled City
Green Zone, Baghdad, Iraq, Monday February 21, 2005

It was a strange feeling to be back in the middle of a war zone again. This time without a uniform, a weapon, or rules of engagement. It was also a strange feeling to be without the legal protection I always had as a member of the U.S. Military. Now as I enter the country I also enter the legal "grey area" that private contractors face in war zones like Iraq. My company alone currently has 35 employees living and working in Iraq. Operation Iraqi Freedom, unlike any other war in U.S. history, has been supported by a massive number of private contractors doing what soldiers used to do. A fact quite clearly spelled out for me by last Wednesday's daily briefing slide at the Joint Operations Center at Camp Arifjan, Kuwait. The slide shows current strength at 160,000 troops, 2,000 Department of Defense employees, and 28,000 private contractors—nearly one contractor for every five soldiers on the ground!

As I walked from the Presidential Palace through the Green Zone to my new office north of the Ibn Sina Hospital I saw many familiar sights. The bombed out buildings, dirty streets, missing drain grates, broken street lights and litter looked all too familiar. Wrinkled, desiccated dates still clung to many of the palm trees from last September. But many things were different too. Aleeya the skinny 8-year old local girl was still panhandling soldiers, but she was now two inches taller and speaking better English. Other sights were not as encouraging.

A tangled mass of twisted steel and rubble was all that remained of the Green Zone Café, blown up by a suicide bomber shortly after I left last October. A deserted dead-end street was all that was left of the once bustling bazaar we called the "Hadji Mart." The most depressing sight to me though, was the number of new $500 apiece 15-foot tall concrete wall panels placed on sidewalks, in parking areas, and in front of almost every occupied building in the once "Green" Zone. The walls in front of Ibn Sina Hospital on both sides of Haifa Street not only eliminated parking and necked down the 4-lane street into two lanes, but required those of us on foot to walk in the street with the traffic. Every compound now had gates, armed guards, and required a special pass to get in. Both vehicles and walkers now had to go through a checkpoint inside the Green Zone and show a pass just to walk to the PX or park in the Palace parking lot. I live and work inside the Green Zone and yet every time I go from my office to dinner I have to show my Embassy pass at no less than three checkpoints.

Open space, parking lots and swimming pools had now been converted to "man-camps" with double-decked shipping containers to live in. Many pine and cedar trees along the boulevards had either been chopped down to make way for concrete walls, or finally succumbed from lack of water for the past two years. Even the traffic has changed, with many fewer old Nissan pickups and Chevy's, and a large increase in fully armored Humvees and SUVs. No, I am not impressed with "progress" in the Green Zone so far. It is unfortunate that the need for security has converted the Green Zone into a walled city of dead-end streets.

Looking south on Haifa Street from the north gate to the Presidential Palace. The "Green Zone" is becoming a city of concrete walls due to the continued lack of security in Baghdad, Iraq. Monday Feb 21, 2005. (Photo DSCN0655/ Dave Conklin)

Polkovnik Kochovski
Presidential Palace, Baghdad, Iraq, Thursday February 24, 2005

I looked up briefly from my breakfast cereal at the Palace dining hall to see an older dark-haired soldier arrive at the opposite side of my table.

He was about my age and size. As he took off his body armor and helmet and placed them over the back of the chair I didn't recognize his camouflage uniform with a NATO patch on his left shoulder. Then he said, "Hi Dave. Did you recognize me without my mustache?" I couldn't believe my eyes. It was Polkovnik (Bulgarian for Colonel) Sergei Kochovski, the Bulgarian Army staff officer I worked with for a year when I was deployed with a military liaison team to Bulgaria in the 1990's. I had not seen Sergei in more than seven years.

I expected to see one or two people I knew maybe, but I never expected to see Sergei again. Sergei was a hard-drinking, fun loving Bulgarian that lived hard, worked hard, and played hard. At one point in his life, while I knew him in Bulgaria, he was going through a difficult divorce and found it difficult to keep away from the hard stuff. Today he seemed to be much more reserved, almost tame, compared to the last time I saw this grizzled war veteran. But he had aged well, and looked much the same as I had known him.

Colonel Sergei Kochovski and Dave Conklin hold a mini-reunion at NATO Headquarters in the Green Zone. Colonel Kochovski was raised in Washington, D.C. spent time in Syria during the last Egyptian-Israeli war, and had been working in the Bulgarian Embassy in Cairo prior to his posting to Iraq as an Arabic translator. Baghdad, Iraq Saturday Jul 23, 2005.
(Photo DSCN1348/ Dave Conklin)

He said he had been in Iraq since last August and would be here for a year or more working for NATO. Previous to that he was in Cairo working out of the Bulgarian Embassy. He speaks fluent Arabic from the time he served in the Palestine (with Egypt) during the Israeli-Egyptian War. He told me he was sent from Cairo to Iraq as a liaison officer and English-Arabic-Bulgarian translator for the coalition here in the Green Zone. He also speaks excellent English, having been raised in Washington, D.C. by his Bulgarian diplomat parents. I wished him well, and we promised to get together again soon and tell war stories one more time.

Death by PowerPoint
Green Zone, Baghdad, Iraq, Thursday February 24, 2005

Today was my first day of training with Aegis Defence Services, one of the defense contractors my employer is supporting with our logistics tracking software. It was scheduled to be a day of death by PowerPoint, but actually turned out to be quite interesting. There were 11 of us to be trained this week. Six who would be assigned to PSDs (Private Security Details) in one of the regional operation centers, the rest who were in administrative positions, and me, of course, who was a subcontractor and not their employee at all. If all goes well I will be the first Field Support Engineer (FSE) in my company authorized to carry a firearm.

Most of the trainees were former military in their thirties from the UK; like Jody, John, and Andy, a former Royal Marine. Michele was from Australia, Chris was from Newcastle, Bardi and Ras were both former South African policemen, and James, a black man from Detroit, was already working security in the Green Zone before this job.

We began with a daily intelligence brief, followed by familiarization with the 9mm Austrian-made Glock pistol. Then each department head came to talk about their operation. But before that, former Brigadier James Ellery, the chief of Aegis-Iraq, talked about the company and the history of the British in Iraq. During World War I the British took Mesopotamia from the Turks but not before losing 24,000 killed in action including 17,000 in one single battle in Al Kut, Iraq. Lawrence of Arabia was part of this campaign, but he and many others were sorely disappointed as to how the Brits carved up the region afterwards.

An insurgency followed (sound familiar?) which collapsed only after it was brutally smashed in 1920 by the Brits with the use of airpower, poison gas, and driving the residents out and burning 16 cities to the ground. A king was installed and monarchy reigned until 1932 when the king was overthrown. "Now," said the Brigadier, "The coalition has not been brutal enough and as a consequence Iraq has become a magnet for insurgents." For example, he pointed out that, "Despite the boldest and cleverest campaign by MG Petraeus in Mosul, it has become an extremely dangerous area." He went on to mention that Tikrit is the center of the Sunni triangle, Baghdad is currently under control but dangerous, Ramadi is full of foreign fighters, and Basrah is full of criminal elements. It was then that I realized that he was talking about his Regional Operations Centers, where I would be installing our new Tapestry Solutions, Inc. logistics tracking computer software. I began to take the five-day indoctrination a little more seriously.

Dave takes aim with an Austrian-made Glock 17 9mm automatic pistol. The Glock 17 has a 17-round magazine. British weapons drills include the commands: Load, Ready, Targets, Stoppage, Magazine, Back-in, Make Safe, and Unload. We practiced weapons drills and dry firing with the Glock pistol, M4 carbine, and AK-47 rifle for five days before qualifying on each weapon. Friday Feb 25, 2005. (Photo DSCN0508/ Dave Conklin

PSD Training
Crossed Sabers Park, Baghdad, Iraq, Saturday February 26, 2005

This morning our PSD training continued. We were told to wear our body armor as we would be doing practical exercises all day. First, however, we received the daily intelligence brief, which included the alarming news that the AIF (Anti-Iraqi Forces) have perfected the making of napalm and are now using some "FA VBIEDs" (fuel-assisted car bombs). Then we all marched outside to the armory and were each issued an M4 carbine and a 9mm Austrian-made Glock pistol. We mounted up in three armored turbocharged diesel Toyota Land Cruisers and headed for the Crossed Sabers Park near the Tomb of the Unknown Iraqi Soldier. This is where many PSCs (Private Security Companies) train their teams.

First we did weapons drills, then driving, then formation driving including U-turn-left, U-turn-right, reverse turn-left hand down, blocking threats from the right and left, and two-point turn-left hand down. We took turns being the client, driver, shooter, team-leader and 2IC (Second In Command) with two to three persons per car. This was followed by more combat first aid and another weapons drill. The armored cars are bulletproof and weigh four tons. Due to the extra weight, they accelerate slowly, are even more top-heavy than normal SUVs and drive like a boat. Swerving and U-turns must be done carefully. Robin Tilley, one of our instructors and a former British Army soldier, said last year he saw a driver overturn and the car catch on fire. Since these cars are armored, you can get trapped easily and you can't break the window to get out!

The only problem we had was when Robin drove into a light pole and dented the front fender. Thank God one of the students didn't do it!

Chris, Andrew, Denny, and John practice moving a wounded client from a disabled vehicle to a rescue car during a simulated ambush drill in Baghdad Saturday Feb 26, 2005. (Photo DSCN0555/ Dave Conklin)

Fully Automatic
Crossed Sabers Park, Baghdad, Iraq, Monday February 28, 2005

The PSD training continued for five days, almost all of it outdoors at the Crossed Sabers Park in the Green Zone. The training included convoy drills, walking formations, and entering and exiting "venue" drills. We practiced a 5-person "diamond" formation for walking clients when dismounted, with three drivers remaining in the vehicles with the engines running. Finally today we put it altogether in convoy drills where the team gets ambushed, has a disabled front, rear, or client vehicle, and has to evacuate, assess, and treat a simulated wounded comrade under fire on foot. In between the PSD drills we practiced weapons drills as well—loading, unloading, clearing, disassembling, and assembling our rifles and pistols.

By late afternoon we were ready for the final test—live fire weapons qualification. We all lined up in front of the weapons room and checked out an M4 carbine, AK-47 and Glock 17. By 3:30 p.m. we were at the shooting range near the south end of the Green Zone. While it was still light outside we fired the Glock. First we were allowed to shoot two times each with 5-rounds to line up our sights. Then to qualify on the Glock we had three 17-round magazines to shoot in the following order:

10 rounds	20 seconds	25 meter target
5 rounds	10 seconds	15 meter target
7 rounds	12 seconds	10 meter target
16 rounds	30 seconds	10 meter target
4 rounds	3 seconds	2 meter target

We then sighted in with the M4 and qualified, all at 25 meters, followed by the AK-47 at 25 meters. With the Kalashnikov (AK) I had forgotten how hard you had to push down on the safety lever to move it from "safe" through "automatic" to the bottom "single shot" position. So when the instructor commanded, "load, ready, targets" instead of firing one round at a time to check my zero, I fired a three-round burst on automatic before I could release the trigger. When I inspected the target I could see my first three rounds, in a neat vertical line, but luckily in the bullseye and all within 2 inches. I have a lot more respect for the AK now.

Michele, Chris, Andrew Denny, James and John clean M4 carbines prior to issuing them for weapons qualification at the ROC compound in Baghdad Monday Feb 28, 2005. (Photo DSCN0618/ Dave Conklin)

13. Back to the Front

When you give your judgment, let it be
with justice and never let your passion interfere.
–Translated Inscription above Presidential Palace Door

Back to Balad
Over Balad, Iraq, Friday March 11, 2005

I was eager to start visiting the six Regional ROCs (Reconstruction Operations Centers) where I would be responsible for their logistics tracking software. Our lead Field Support Engineer (FSE) Mark Christy, a former Green Beret, had been to almost all of them and installed their software. Now it was my job under this contract to keep the systems maintained, install upgrades as they are released, and train the operators on how to use the Tapestry Solutions, Inc. GDMS (Global Distribution Management System) computer application to its full potential.

The rain had finally quit today so Mark came to me and said,

Why don't you try for a Space-A helo flight to Balad to talk with Ken Croston on developing a training plan? Then if you can, catch a flight to Diwaniyah or Ramadi to get their systems maintained and upgraded — and by the way, if you can figure out how to get to these places, draw up some maps and travel directions for next time. I want us to get someone out to each of these centers once a month if we can.

So I was able to catch an afternoon flight to Balad and spent the evening installing software and maintaining some systems there with Brian Prather, our Iraq country manager. The next morning I "waded" to the training trailer and met with Ken on training and by noon I was back at "Catfish Air" on my way to Camp Victory to make my first regional ROC visit. The day was clear as we flew back over Baghdad. The scene below was one of a million shallow lakes as the rain had nowhere to go on this flat plain between the Tigris and Euphrates Rivers. Fields, streets, garbage dumps, and housing areas all were surrounded by shallow lakes. Soon with warmer weather this would become a breeding ground for mosquitoes with malaria and dysentery. Any soft surface would mire a truck if driven on. This was a desert not made of sand.

I soon arrived at Camp Victory and slogged my way to the ROC where I met all the staff and worked on their computer until after midnight.

A Humvee sits stranded in the mud at Camp Victory on the western edge of Baghdad after two days and nights of rain. Saturday Mar 12, 2005. (Photo DSCN0675/ Dave Conklin)

The Wake of Alan Parker
Green Zone, Baghdad, Iraq, Thursday April 21, 2005

On Thursday evenings in the Aegis compound there is usually a lot of cheer and merriment in the patio as the PSDs and staff blow off some steam after a tense week on the streets of Baghdad. Not so tonight. Sure there was the usual crowd and the usual beer and pretzels, but the mood was not at all cheerful. Big strong men, former British paratroopers from the 7th Parachute Regiment Royal Horse Artillery, had hung their regimental flag over the bar and were drinking—and crying.

One of the car bombs on Route Irish today claimed the life of their teammate Alan Parker. I saw him with his team in the parking lot only this morning, a big man himself, with tattoos on his arms and always a smile on his face. He was a gunner in the back of an armored Toyota in a three-car convoy escorting a VIP on the airport road. A suicide bomber drove from the right lane in between the middle and lead cars and blew himself up. Another man was severely burned but lived only because he was blown out of the car by the blast. It happened at 9:03 a.m. –I know because I monitor the Tapestry computer system that was tracking his vehicle, AE005, when it stopped sending a signal at that time. There was no time to press the panic alarm. Everything happened too fast.

Al Jazeera News reported the incident as follows:

> Contractors killed--Also on Thursday a bomb targeting Western workers in Iraq exploded, killing a security contractor. A spokeswoman for the Great Britain-based Aegis Defence Services said one employee was killed and another injured as their car headed from the capital towards the airport. "Aegis Defence Services can confirm that one member of staff was killed in the line of duty in Baghdad today and another person sustained injuries," she said. She gave no details as to their identities. Aljazeera reported the two were U.S. citizens. One Iraqi civilian, travelling in another car, was also hurt by the blast, according to an interior ministry official.
>
> Aljazeera also reported an explosion caused by a car bomb targeting a U.S. convoy near al-Amil neighborhood. Iraqi journalist Muhammad Abd Allah told Aljazeera an Iraqi driver was also wounded in the attack and was transferred to a nearby hospital. "No other casualties were immediately reported, but one of the vehicles was consumed by flames, and white smoke rose from another one," police Captain Hamid Ali said. All three vehicles appeared to have been blown off the road by the impact of the explosion, witnesses said. The road to the airport is only a few kilometers long and flanked by U.S. military bases. The U.S. Army labelled it as "Route Irish." But Abd Allah said Airport Road was known as *al Matar* or "Death Road."

Later the same day I heard that insurgents shot down a civilian Bulgarian helicopter with eight Blackwater Security Contractors on board. Posted on a website the next day was a video of them gunning down the wounded Bulgarian pilot. I don't know the Blackwater guys, but I do know that the Alan Parker who died today was 45 years old, had been married for 20 years and had three children

The remains of an armored Toyota Land Cruiser after a VBIED pulled out of the middle lane of Baghdad's notorious Airport Highway to detonate between the first and second vehicles as they passed in the left hand lane. The Toyota was severely damaged, set on fire and came to rest in the median with one person dead and one badly injured. The second vehicle also had significant damage including two blown front tires. Thursday Apr 21, 2005. (VBIED) (Photo – Aegis)

14. Spring Travels

Take care not to oppress anyone. It is better for you to wrongfully punish someone rather than . . . live your life regretting for oppressing someone.
 – Translated Inscription above Presidential Palace Door

The Transition Season
Kuwait International Airport, Kuwait, Tuesday May 24, 2005
    The "Kuwit Pocket Guide" calls this month the transition month between spring and "early dry hot summer" which precedes "late humid hot summer." What that means in practical terms is that when my plane from Amsterdam touched down at Kuwait International Airport this evening at 10:55 p.m. the temperature was 38 degrees Celsius, or 100 degrees Fahrenheit. So you can add "acclimatization" to the ten time zone jet lag I was feeling right now. Only twenty-four hours ago I had boarded a plane in Kalispell, Montana, after two weeks of R&R (rest and recuperation) leave which I spent with my family in Cabo San Lucas, Mexico. As soon as my flight left Kalispell, I was able to look down at my favorite fishing lake—still iced over with snow covering the surrounding landscape in late May.
    Frank Montini, one of our Tapestry guys in Kuwait, was at the airport taking another guy to catch a plane to his daughter's graduation, and picking me up. Frank is an ex-cop from Cleveland, Ohio, and is a storyteller. He joined the company last December just after I did. Last year he was working security for CSA Associates in Kuwait so he knows his way around here which is very helpful.
    Now that I have been to the Kuwait Airport a few times I was getting to like it. First of all, it's not too huge and it's air-conditioned. Climate control is very helpful in these transition seasons. Secondly, I realized that the airport between the check-in counters and the gates is basically a two-story shopping mall. Not only do they have jewelry, electronics, banks, and a food court with a Cinnabon café, but also a Starbucks coffee house on each floor. By the way, did I mention that while you are having your cappuccino you can also check your e-mail on their free wireless internet service?
    Frank wanted to get a haircut at the 24-hour barbershop so I decided to get one too. Ramar, one of the local barbers, told me that for four KD's (Kuwaiti Dinars - about twelve U.S. dollars), you can get a standard haircut. So I proceeded to find out what a standard haircut was. Arabs must be very hairy people, or think they are, because I found out that a

standard haircut in the Arab world means removing hair not only from the top of your head, but also from every bump, crack and opening on your head as well.

The central area of the Kuwait International Airport has two levels of shops and cafes including two Starbucks coffee shops with free wireless internet access. Monday May 9, 2005. (DSCN0900) (Photo -- Dave Conklin)

First the haircut. Done very well with razor cut sideburns and neck. But just when I thought he was done Ramar had a surprise for me. He wrapped a piece of tissue around the end of a pair of scissors, soaked it in lighter fluid and lit it with a cigarette lighter as if it were a candle. After saying "Happy Birthday," he proceeded to pass the "torch" all around each of my ears, burning off any stray hairs until my ears were as smooth as a baby's. Well, I figured that didn't hurt so I guess no harm done.

"Now was I done?" No not yet. Next Ramar took a Q-tip swab and stuck the end in a bowl of hot wax. "Now what could that be for?" Soon I had a Q-tip with hot wax on one end shoved up my nose! Then I had another shoved up the other nostril. I was hoping that there wasn't any hair in my mouth or I wouldn't be able to breathe. I was thinking, "I'm glad no one has a camera," as I sat there staring into the barber's mirror with two Q-tips sticking out of my nose like overgrown cat whiskers. Then without warning, Ramar grabbed one and jerked it out, proudly showing me how much hair he was able to capture. After he jerked out the second one I was sure I had no more hair to give, but then he started in on my eyebrows. Luckily I still have a thin line of hair left as he only "trimmed" them. Finally Ramar asked if I wanted a shampoo treatment. Now being afraid that there must be some kind of hair remover in the shampoo as well, I told him I would love to but really needed to give my seat up so my friend Frank would not have to wait any longer to get his "standard haircut."

The Price of Gas
Kuwait City, Kuwait, Wednesday May 25, 2005

Frank drove me back to his apartment in the company's rented Mitsubishi SUV. Despite sleeping only five hours, I was up by 7:00 a.m., walked around the corner to the café and bought an omelet breakfast for 1.50 KD (about $4.50). After breakfast I rousted Frank to drive me to the PWC (Public Warehouse Company) logistics center in Kuwait City. PWC is Kuwaiti owned and one of the largest transport companies in this part of the world. I was going to catch a ride with one of their guys for the hour and a half drive to the port of Umm Qasr just across the border in Iraq, where PWC has a large receiving and shipping compound. For the next two days I would be loading our GDMS (Global Distribution Management System) software onto computers here and at Khor AzZubayr, another Iraqi port about 20 km further north.

Frank was almost out of fuel so we stopped at one of the gas stations that dot the freeways here. Today there was a line at the pumps and a longer line at the cash window at the exit. While we were waiting, I asked Frank about the price of gas. "Well," he said, "The Kuwaitis were giving it away to the Coalition military for free up until April. Now they passed a law that the military has to pay for fuel as well." But since fuel was measured in liters and the price in KDs, Frank wasn't sure how it translated into dollars. So I decided to find out. We put 57 liters into the 74 liter Mitsubishi SUV fuel tank. Frank paid 3.40 KD to fill it up. Today the exchange rate is 3.42 KD per 1.00 USD. So if you cipher all that out, Frank paid the equivalent of $11.63 for 15 gallons of gas at the Kuwaiti retail price of $0.78 per gallon. That sure beats the $2.49 per gallon I paid in Spokane, Washington, last week. No wonder the Kuwaitis love big Chevy Suburbans and fast sports cars.

A Visit to "Kozy Bear"
Port of Khor AzZubayr, Iraq, Thursday May 26, 2005

Jamie White, the PWC safety manager, and I drove north in a new Ford diesel 3/4 ton pickup along the Kuwaiti coast until we reached the border of Iraq at what is called the "U.N. Crossing." Here between Kuwait and Iraq is a 100 meter no-man's land with chain link fences topped with razor wire on each end. We pulled up to the Kuwait gate and waited until someone in the guardhouse pushed the button on the automatic gate. Then we drove ahead to the Iraq border. The station was manned by a single Iraqi soldier who looked at our CAC ID cards, looked inside the truck, and then opened the single pole that served as a gate. We drove through to a waiting armored car with a PSD team of Fiji Islanders employed by PWC. We transferred to the armored car and the others followed us in our pickup for the short drive through the village of Umm Qasr to the port less than a mile away. The port is fenced and guarded and the PWC compound inside the port is also fenced and guarded by PWC security personnel, mostly Fijians.

The next day I loaded the software and trained the warehouse manager on how to operate it. Then Chris, their PSD chief and his Fijians drove me up to my next job at the port of Khor Az Zubayr, or "Kozy Bear" as the Brits call it. As we drove north through the flat desert landscape on the two-lane highway I looked to the east and thought I saw a mirage. There, only a mile or two away, in the middle of the desert, were two huge cargo ships. Then I realized that they were in the bay, but the landscape was too flat to see the water around them.

Four thousand Chevy cars and four-door mini pickup trucks with light bars wait at the Iraqi Port of Khor Az Zubayr for onward movement and distribution to Iraqi police forces. The port, run by the Iraqi government, is 20 kilometers north of the Port of Umm Qasr. Thursday May 26, 2005. (DSCN1088) (Photo --Dave Conklin)

When we reached the port, two ships docked there were already disgorging vehicles to add to the 4,000 police cars now in the PWC compound. Two thousand more had already been shipped north. After I finished my work, I was supposed to get a ride to my next job in the city of Basrah, but I noticed that the PSD team had left. My PWC contact here was Dale, a "Kiwi" from New Zealand. He said they were called out on another mission so I would have to spend the night. So I made myself at home in a small trailer room they gave me then went for a run around the compound. After my run I climbed one of the light towers for a better view of the port. It was a quiet night and I got up early the next morning for the 45-minute drive to the Basrah Airport.

Back from Basrah
Baghdad International Airport, Iraq, Saturday May 28, 2005

The RAF (Royal Air Force) has a daily flight between Basrah, Baghdad and Kuwait City and you can make a reservation and know that you have a seat when you arrive at the airport. So after I was done with my work at the Iraqi ports of Umm Qasr, Khor AzZubayr and Basrah, I was at the Basrah Airport at the appointed show time of 7:00 a.m. Then me and about 50 British soldiers waited—and waited—for the flight in the stifling 100 degree-plus heat of the second floor airport waiting room. Our cargo plane was parked outside, a Hercules C-130 J model which is wider, longer and faster than the H models the Americans are using here. The easiest way to tell the J from the H model is by the six-blade propellers.

Unfortunately, today its "heads-up" display was not working. At 10:30 a.m. they announced the problem was fixed and we were to put our "carry-ons" through the X-ray machine. I'm not sure why they have an X-ray machine because all the soldiers and myself had guns, knives, cans of mace and body armor that were all put through and given back to us. I even had to take the change out of my pockets before I went through the X-ray door.

Finally at 11:00 a.m. we were "wheels up" and happy to be high above the desert where the air was cooler, even if there were no windows to see out. I sat next to two journalists heading to Dubai to catch a 14-hour plane ride back to Australia. They had been doing stories on the Australia Brigade north of Basrah. We landed without incident at BIAP (Baghdad International Airport). Waiting there at the gate to catch a flight out to Kuwait were our company's trainers from Virginia –Shane Culbreth and

Anthony Moser. They had been in Iraq now for about two months and had been able to visit a lot of places as well as spend all of May in Baghdad giving weekly 40-hour training courses to the Aegis watchkeepers on how to operate the GDMS software. This was a big help to us since Mark Christy and I were always busy with day-to-day maintenance and troubleshooting in six locations throughout Iraq.

Now the training was done and they were on their way home before their next assignment. I was glad to see them one more time before they left.

From left: Shane Culbreth, Dave Conklin and Anthony Moser at the Baghdad International Airport (BIAP) military passenger terminal just before Shane's and Anthony's RAF flight to Kuwait International Airport. Saturday May 28, 2005. (DSCN1098) (Photo --Dave Conklin)

15. Summer Attacks

*Your conscience and your mind are your sultan
and not your tongue or your passion.*
– Translated Inscription above Presidential Palace Door

Night Moves
2nd Marine Expeditionary Force, Camp Fallujah, Iraq, Sunday May 29, 2005

My next destination was Fallujah. Since my last visit to Ramadi, the Reconstruction Operations Center had been moved to Fallujah at the Second Marine Expeditionary Camp. Like the rocket attack just before I landed at Ramadi last March, I was sure that I would find something interesting going on in Fallujah too, especially since this was Abu Zarqawi's headquarters last year and Operation Lightning was just launched to drive hundreds of insurgents out of nearby Baghdad.

Like Ramadi, most of the military flights and ground convoys come here only at night. Mark Christy and I knew the logistics movement control coordinator at Fallujah, Marine Gunnery SGT Dale Swink. He was able to manifest me along with four Pakistanis headed to Camp Fallujah to work at the Burger King there. The night was clear and quiet and I could track our convoy's direction by watching the big dipper constellation.

I spent the night, or what was left of it, in the Aegis trailer camp and started upgrading their computer application the next morning. At their morning PSD brief they went over a plan for four SUVs with 14 total passengers to take a team of Army Engineers to check the progress of construction on a couple of police stations in the north part of the city of Fallujah. Then they got in their armored Toyota Land Cruisers and took off.

About 10:30 a.m. as I was working with the watchkeeper, Grahame Tearle, I heard someone on the radio bark, "contact left, contact right, oh shit contact front." Something was definitely going down. Next, the Tapestry GDMS computer system I was working on received a panic alarm from AE016, one of their vehicles. For the next five minutes or so things were tense and information was limited. We had the Marines on the other channel when we heard a voice on the radio say, "We are OK, no QRF (quick reaction force) needed.

Apparently the PSD convoy turned onto a street in Fallujah with a U.S. Marine observation post (OP) at the end which they did not see. As they approached it, the Marines thought they might be suicide bombers, and popped a flare then opened up on them from the OP and the roofs of nearby buildings with their M249 machine guns. The PSD, not knowing who is firing, speeds up and heads for the Marine checkpoint down the street past the OP. Then seeing the OP firing, the Marines at the checkpoint also open up on them with their machine gun. Finally the PSD turns around, runs the gauntlet past the OP again, turns the corner and keeps on going with the Marines shooting at them until they are out of range.

After reaching another checkpoint, the PSD team does a damage assessment, changes their flat tires with the few spares that aren't shot up, and limps back to base on their remaining run-flat tires. I checked out the four vehicles when they returned and they had over 100 rounds fired into them and four flat tires. The lead and rear vehicles were hit the most with 22 rounds in the front windshield of the lead vehicle alone. Two bullets came through the roof of the rear vehicle but missed all inside.

Luckily all 14 had miraculously survived this Blue-on-Blue "friendly fire" incident. The episode was another example of incomplete communication and poor procedures—just what the terrorists want. For example the PSD team is required to file a movement plan 48 hours ahead with the Marines. Neither the plan, the information, nor the numbers and types of vehicles were given to the checkpoint nor the OP. Neither the PSD nor the Marines are allowed to monitor each other's radio frequencies so they could not call a cease fire. Finally, the Marines had been alerted that insurgents were trying to locate vehicles like those used by PSDs to use as car bombs.

The next day I finished up my work as the team was doing a thorough "lessons learned" review. I thanked them again for always making my visits to their camp interesting, then headed back to Baghdad.

Two members of the PSD team stand next to the 22 direct hits taken on the windshield of the lead vehicle in Sunday's Blue-on-Blue friendly fire incident in the city of Fallujah. The Marines fired over one-hundred rounds into the four armored Toyota Land Cruisers. Sunday May 29, 2005.

(DSCN1104) (Photo --Dave Conklin)

Things that go Boom in the Night
Green Zone Café, Bagdad, Saturday June 4, 2005

Yesterday went as planned, which was unusual in itself. This was also the day I finally arrived back in Baghdad after being gone exactly one month --on leave in Mexico, then installing software in Iraq. After I got back from Fallujah I had to fly back to Basrah again to reinstall some software for MAJ Beloney, the 484th MCB liaison officer stationed at Multi-National Division Southeast (MND-SE) at the Basrah Airport. On my return trip my RAF flight landed at BIAP on time and I was met by Carl from Aegis who took me to their operations center at Camp Victory where I put their system on a stand-alone domain while their server was being repaired. Then after dinner I was able to catch a Blackhawk helicopter flight to the Green Zone.

I landed at 9:30 p.m. and met my counterpart Mark Christy behind the Palace for a situation update. Our conversation was punctuated by a couple of loud booms which we judged to be mortar rounds nearby. A minute or two later, as usual, the palace loud speaker announced "take cover" as if it would do any good after the fact.

This morning I read in the Stars and Stripes Newspaper that the Iraqi government put the first official count of Iraqis killed by insurgents at 12,000 since the war began. To make matters worse, it is estimated that 825 people have been killed here in the month since the new government was announced on April 28th. And from another perspective, last year 130 car bombs were detonated in Iraq. Last month alone over 130 car bombs were detonated in Iraq.

So for a brief moment I thought about all the close calls I had recently. For example I saw an intelligence briefing today that said two rockets had hit LZ (Landing Zone) Washington in the Green Zone last night, about 15 minutes after I had landed (hmm, the two "booms" last night). Last Sunday night I stopped at the North Victory PX before I left for Fallujah. Outside in the patio a crowd was watching nightly showings of the new Star Wars movie on a big screen. Little did I know that word got to the insurgents who a night or two later fired 120mm rockets into the crowd killing one soldier and wounding twenty more from the Kentucky National Guard.

WAITING FOR A BUS MAY BE DANGEROUS – DON'T STAND OUT <u>DEAD</u> IN THE <u>OPEN</u>

Subject:
THREAT WARNING T038:AIF Access to Sniper Rifles in Baghdad

THREAT WARNING T038

Recent reporting would suggest that insurgents have access to sniper rifles in the Baghdad area. We must be mindful of personal security measures, even within the International Zone. It is not recommended standing around in exposed areas having casual conversation.

You are also advised to wear your Body armour and helmet when outdoors.

Even waiting for a bus in the gated, guarded, and Coalition controlled Green Zone can be hazardous to your health according to this sign posted at the bus stop in front of the PCO compound next to Ibn Sina Hospital. It seems to be just another oxymoron of war when they build bus stops then post signs telling you not to use them. Friday Apr 22, 2005. (DSCN0859) (Photo --Dave Conklin)

At Fallujah I could have just as easily asked to go with the PSD team that was shot up by the Marines on their short mission within the city. Even yesterday when I was at Camp Victory working on their computers I heard several booms that sounded like artillery to the north. They turned out to be a mortar attack on the gymnasium at North Victory that killed one soldier and wounded three others. Now I sit here in the rebuilt Green Zone Café sipping on a Jack Daniels and Coke, wondering where the suicide bomber was sitting last October when he demolished himself and the entire café. But I do not dwell on these thoughts. No one should really. Life is too surreal and tenuous here to want to think about these things much.

Attack at Habbaniyah
Logistics Movement Coordination Center, Green Zone, Tuesday June 7, 2005

A normal day for me could mean answering or asking questions by e-mail or phone, monitoring the internet data feeds that provide civilian convoy tracking throughout Iraq, doing computer software installations, maintenance, and training workstation operators. But today would be anything but normal.

I am temporarily sharing office space at the LMCC (Logistics Movement Coordination Center) in the PCO (Projects & Contracting Office) compound in the Green Zone. When I came in at 7:30 a.m. Mark was already monitoring the internet feed and noticed that one of the satellite transponder systems was not working. We notified the company immediately. This meant that we could not track about fifty transponders on the road today. That could equate to over 300 vehicles with no overwatch.

Security details also have cell phones, radios and GPS (Global Positioning System) receivers as backups, but they do not always work. I know that because each security company has a liaison person here at the LMCC who monitors their movement and can call for help if they get into trouble, and more than once our GDMS software has told us where PSDs were being attacked up to 20 minutes before they could contact the liaison person here by radio or phone. We were nervous because in a worst case scenario a convoy could come under attack, send a panic alarm, and without a satellite feed, we could not tell the military where to send a Quick Reaction Force (QRF) to help them if the PSD couldn't talk to us— and lot of people could die. Today would be that worst case scenario.

A convoy of ten trucks and five PSD vehicles was headed west past Fallujah when their transponder quit sending position updates. So did all one hundred transponders that were using this same satellite. Then, at about 11:20 a.m. Dan the convoy liaison at the LMCC here received an animated call on his cellphone from Joe, a PSD commander. The volume on the 2-way radio was loud enough for me to overhear the conversation. The next 30 minutes sounded something like you could only imagine if you had been with General George Custer at the Little Bighorn.

We will never know if Joe tried to send a panic alarm because the transponder was not working. Joe tried to explain what was going on to Dan. Apparently the ambush first stopped the lead vehicle, then took out the rear vehicle and then attackers closed in from both sides of the road. Dan kept shouting over the shooting, "Joe, Joe what's your location." But Joe had no time to look at a map, only to talk and shoot. Joe said, "There are fields and palm trees nearby." Then he described the battle and as the attackers closed in I could hear over the cell phone the "pop-pop-pop" of automatic rifles getting louder and more frequent. Dan told Joe that the QRF had been called and was on its way--but to where exactly? Would the military arrive in time to save them? I felt helpless and sick inside as I listened and waited.

After a few more minutes Joe said, "We're being overrun." "I am almost out of ammunition, I have been shot in the arm, I have to put the phone down." Joe did not speak again, but the shooting was getting louder—then it stopped. After a few minutes we heard voices again—but this time they were in Arabic. Dan quickly got his translator to listen in. Voices were discussing in Arabic whether to take Joe hostage or to shoot him. Then the sound of a vehicle moving. Then nothing but silence. The attack was over in 35 minutes. I looked at my watch. It was 11:55 a.m.

By the time the QRF could locate the battle and arrive armed and ready, all they found were nine bodies and fifteen burning vehicles. Twelve additional escorts and drivers including Joe were missing, and some were later found dead. That night one of the wounded who had been flown to the Combat Support Hospital here with a face wound, came over and told us how he had managed to survive.

This man said the team was only carrying 120 rounds of ammunition per person. When he ran out of ammo, he saw an AK rifle next to one of his fallen comrades and ran to pick it up. When he got there he discovered the magazine was empty. So he dove into a nearby ditch then low-crawled away out of sight until he found a culvert. He hid there until the soldiers arrived.

Could someone have saved Joe and his men if their transponder had been working so we could give the Marine QRF an exact position? No one will ever know, but I hope I never have to ask that question again.

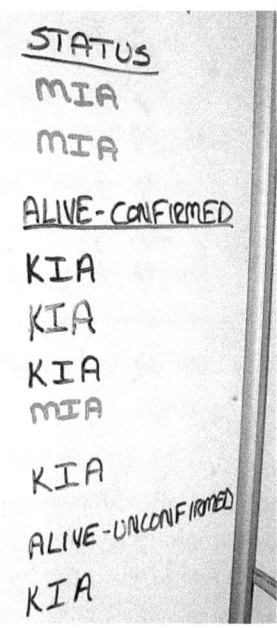

This whiteboard in our office in Baghdad lists the status of ten truck drivers (names not shown) on the ill-fated convoy that was attacked and overrun near the town of Habbaniyah. Another whiteboard lists the names and status of nineteen members of the security team. Of the 29 personnel, only five were found alive. No one will erase the boards until all are accounted for—one way or the other. Thursday Jun 9, 2005. (DSCN1157) (Photo --Dave Conklin)

Happy Independence Day
Projects and Contracting Office, Green Zone, Monday July 4, 2005

We have a lot to be thankful for, even here in Baghdad. A couple of days ago our Air Force and Army logistics guys took CPT Mike Ewer to the airport to fly back to Lackland Air Force Base in Texas after his 4-month deployment. On the way back they stopped at the Abu Ghraib warehouse, but didn't leave until about 6:30 p.m. I try never to be on the roads here after 5 p.m. so I was worried about them. Sure enough, at 7 p.m. they sent a panic alarm from their transponder and called in that they were being shot at.

When they returned, they inspected their armored Suburban. It looks like armor-piercing bullets were used because the bullets went through the back door steel plate and into the back seat cushions. Also in the back seat was our new Air Force "LT" who had only been here a week. A lot of merchandise in the back has bullet holes in it but no one was hurt and we are all thankful.

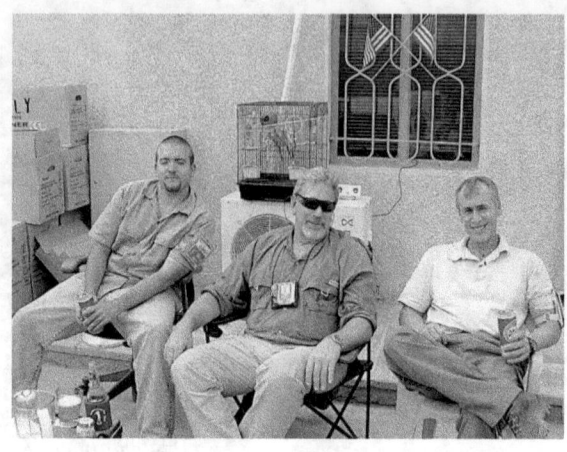

Lewis Byrd, Bob Hayden, and Kent Aldridge (L to R), civilian contractors who work with the Defense Department's Projects & Contracting Office (PCO) enjoy a warm Independence Day Barbeque in front of the PCO-Logistics office during a sandstorm in the Green Zone, Baghdad, Iraq. Monday Jul 4, 2005. (DSCN1283) (Photo --Dave Conklin)

So today we had a little Independence Day BBQ here during a dust storm—rough on the eyes but the wind made the flags fly nicely. Since the temperature was about 107 F, we didn't even need to put the hot dogs in the oven to keep them warm!

God Bless America and our Soldiers and Veterans!

Republic Day
Freedom Building, Green Zone, Thursday July 14, 2005

Although Iraq attained its independence from Great Britain as a kingdom in 1932, the last king was deposed and a "republic" was proclaimed by the first of Iraq's series of military strongmen on July 14, 1958. This date, as do all anniversary dates here, provide more excuses for indiscriminate bombing and killing by armed terrorists. So I was expecting that possibility this Thursday.

The day began with another hot, dusty, dirty *"haboob"* (sandstorm) blowing through with air so thick I could look at the sun without squinting. Before 8:00 a.m. I could hear scattered machine gun fire in the distance. Then at 8:58 a.m. as I waited for the daily ROC intelligence briefing to begin, the windows of the Freedom Building rattled from one, then two explosions. Every checkpoint to the Green Zone has been hit at one time or another by car bombs. Today it was no less than three suicide bombers at Checkpoint 2 near the Al Rasheed Hotel. First a car bomber exploded himself, then a suicide bomber on foot blew himself up. The third bomber was also on foot and decided to run away but was shot and captured. Shortly afterwards I got a call from an Iraqi businessman, who I was supposed to meet at 10:00 a.m. Ahmed said he would be late because they had closed all the checkpoints to the Green Zone. He said he was only 60 meters from the car bomb when it went off.

In the meantime we got a panic alarm on our computer screens from a convoy to the airport on Route Irish, the infamous "Death Road." They were delivering supplies and when they turned onto Irish someone in a car stopped on the overpass and began shooting at their last vehicle from the rear. They kept going and delivered their supplies and their wounded to the hospital at Camp Victory.

The sandstorm was still blowing and the temperature was 119 F outside but Ahmed managed to go all the way around to Checkpoint 11 and finally got into the Green Zone. I met him at 1:30 p.m. I was showing him our computer system when Mike from the LMCC Comtech team burst in the door and yelled, "EVERYONE OUT, EVACUATE THE BUILDING NOW." He said that "Sniffy" the bomb sniffing dog smelled traces of explosives on a red car that was in the entry bay to the compound. It could be another potential VBIED so we were all sent over to the Freedom Building and waited for the EOD guys. In the meantime, Ahmed and I found a corner with a couple of chairs and had our meeting in the middle of the crowd.

Now Ahmed was late for his next meeting because security wouldn't let us out until EOD determined that the traces of explosives that the dog smelled on the car were not a bomb. How does EOD do this? It's simple; they blow up the car and see if there is a secondary explosion. In this case, there was only one boom, so no car bomb. On my way back to the building Andy Gough, one of the PSD guys and a real joker, asked if I had seen his red car anywhere. I said "If it's the one with the bulge in the roof, I think they are towing it down the street right now."

A shiny red Korean armored car, previously worth about $80,000 sits in the PCO compound entrance bay after having been blown to pieces by the Explosive Ordinance Detachment to determine whether it had been rigged as a car bomb. Thursday Jul 14, 2005. (DSC01786) (Photo -- Kent Aldridge)

The Big Shamal
Green Zone, Baghdad, Iraq, Monday August 8, 2005

The dust alarm went off at about 4:00 a.m. outside my room. Every building in the compound had a smoke alarm to alert us in case of fire. But I call them "dust alarms" rather than smoke alarms as I have never seen smoke as thick as the dust here. At first the alarm cycled on and off. But by the time I got out of bed at 7:00 a.m. it was ringing continuously. I knew it would be dusty outside, but when I looked out the window, I could hardly see the next building only 50 meters away. I turned off my air conditioner and closed my bathroom vent to keep as much of the dust out of the room as possible while I was at work.

As dust storms or *shamals* go, this one was a doozy. I put my hat and Wiley-X sunglasses on as usual, but also grabbed my trusty neckerchief, soaked it in water and tied it over my face. My sunglasses have closefitting lenses to keep out the dust, and I can use clear lenses on dark days like this. Today the sky was a dark orange and there was no hint as to where the sun might be. Even cars had to use their headlights to see. It was as if a large volcano had erupted nearby. When the cars drove by, their tires left tracks in the dust and the wind blew the dust into little piles. I was reminded of a Montana blizzard except that this stuff was not going to melt away. I even asked LTC Jose Velazquez, an Army logistics officer that I work with, to make a dust angel so I could take his picture. He of course refused.

Not only were airplanes and helicopters grounded but the shuttle buses were cancelled and local workers who worked outside were sent home. We cancelled a number of supply convoys as there was no QRF or air support available today in the event they were attacked. The rest of us cleaned out our air conditioners, put on dust masks and continued to work. Soon everything in my office, on my desk, even in my desk drawers was covered with a thin film of red dust. At 9:00 a.m. I walked over to the Freedom Building for the daily intelligence briefing, taking movie pictures of the storm along the way. When I reached the guardhouse I went up to the Gurkha guard and showed him my photo ID badge as usual. But then I thought, "How could he tell me from anybody else today? I have on a baseball cap, wrap-around sunglasses, and a mask over my face. Heck today everybody looks like a terrorist."

Inside the building you could see the dust hanging in the air and forming a film on anything flat. The light coming from the projector lens was even highlighted in the dusty briefing room. Many of those who came for the briefing were also wearing dust masks. On the way back to my office every bush or door I bumped into dumped a layer of dust on my shirt. Later every hour or so back in the office I would wipe off my computer, wash the dust off my hands and cough up a gob of silt. "Look on the bright side," LTC Velazquez said, "At least the temperature is only 102 F today." "Uh, huh." By sunset we could again see at least the outline of the sun. We were both hoping that the dust alarms would be silent tomorrow.

Army LTC Jose Velazquez and Dave Conklin stand on Haifa Street in Baghdad's Green Zone during one of the worst sandstorms in many years according to locals. Monday Aug 8, 2005. (DSCN1392) (Photo --Dave Conklin)

16. Prelude to Ramadan

When you are not attending the field of work and action for a reasonable cause, never let your shadow be absent...
– Translated Inscription above Presidential Palace Door

Bad Day in Basrah
Basrah International Airport, Iraq, Monday September 19, 2005

This would be my third and last day in Basrah for this visit, and it turned out to be a good thing too because Basrah was quickly losing its reputation as one of the safest cities in Iraq. I had four computers to install new software releases on at the Basrah Airport so I didn't need to drive anywhere. Recently I heard on world news that four civilian contractors were killed in Basrah. When Henrich Osten from Hart Group picked me up at the Aegis Defence Services Reconstruction Operations Center and drove me to the Hart compound at the Airport I asked him who was killed.

6-1. *A young Iraqi girl poses in her best dress at the Navistar crossing into Kuwait near the border town of Safwan about a one-hour drive from Basrah, the second largest city in Iraq. Monday Aug 29, 2005. (DSCN1470) (Photo --Dave Conklin)*

Heinrich said that four Triple Canopy guys in one vehicle were killed by a command detonated IED. It happened on the expressway turnoff just outside the airport. They had turned off and were on the overpass when the IED placed on a guardrail went off and blew them and their armored car off the overpass and onto the highway below. Henrich didn't know if the four, all in one armored car, were killed by the IED or the resulting fall off the bridge—but I guess it doesn't really matter does it?

So my dreams of having dinner in downtown Basrah were dashed for the foreseeable future and the next morning I took the daily RAF flight back to Baghdad. Back in my office I learned a valuable lesson on Operational Security (OPSEC). I told my wife Mary that I would be in Basrah for a few days and would call her when I returned. She already found it nerve-racking to listen to world news and began taking medication to calm her nerves. So when she heard that four civilian contractors had just been killed in Basrah she thought it was me. She said she was so scared that she began screaming and didn't know what to do. When I called her as promised, she was so surprised to hear my voice that she could not stop crying. After that I only told her where I was going AFTER I got back.

Beyond Najaf
Reconstruction Operations Center, Camp Echo, Diwaniyah, Iraq, Tuesday October 4, 2005

I heard that the weekly helo flight from Balad south would stop in the Green Zone after lunch before going to Camp Echo in the city of Diwaniyah in Central Iraq. For months I had been promising Tim and Derek, watchkeepers at the ROC (Reconstruction Operations Center) there, that I would come and visit soon, so now I could make good on that promise. I almost always go "space-A" and almost always get a seat. I called earlier and was told that the flight was full, but after waiting for two hours and then two more for a maintenance problem, space became available and I was manifested for the hour-long flight.

Another car bomb rattled the walls of the flight ops trailer as I was waiting for the helos to arrive. I later heard that this bomb killed 3 Iraqi policemen just outside Checkpoint 2 at the north end of the Green Zone. I went outside and could see the black smoke from the burning vehicle, then phoned my colleague Mark Christy to make sure he and co-worker Mike were accounted for.

Finally we were on our way. On the way down the machine gunner blazed away at a shallow lake below—just for practice of course. People waved to us as we passed over the date palm groves, green fields, and deserts. The pilot flew low, passing next to water towers and cliff edges, going up and then quickly down when a power line was in our path. It was a fun flight—if you like roller coasters. Soon we flew over a gigantic cemetery near a gold-domed mosque and landed at a small helipad in a city near the Euphrates which I later found out was Najaf.

The afternoon sun chases our Blackhawk helicopter shadow over the Muslim cemetery north of the gold-domed Mosque at Najaf, Iraq. One of the largest and most sacred cemeteries of Islam, burial crypts stretch into the horizon as far as the eye can see. Tuesday Oct 4, 2005. (DSCN1593) (Photo --Dave Conklin)

Camp Echo is the headquarters of the Multinational Division in Central Iraq, run by the Polish with support from just about everybody else including Sweden and Bulgaria so I shouldn't have been surprised to see Russian-made Hip and Hind helicopters on the tarmac when we landed. I with three others from the Green Zone got off there and I asked how they were getting back. They said they had a flight back scheduled for tomorrow so I asked what time and said I would see them there, space-A as usual.

I had a small sketch map of where I needed to go so I picked up my rucksack and headed down the street. Luckily the first checkpoint I got to was manned by two Bulgarian soldiers and since I speak Bulgarian I was able to ask them for directions. Of course they were quite surprised; but I was even more surprised that I could understand their answers.

Later that night at about 10 p.m. when I finished my work on their computer I walked over to my bunk in the Marine Corps compound. Glen from the ROC and some other guys were sitting outside around a large fire drinking beer and throwing in a wood pallet from time to time to keep the flame going. They asked me to join them so I did for a short time. But after going to bed at 4:30 a.m. and getting up at 7:00 a.m. this morning I was a bit tired and soon turned in for the night.

Back from Camp Echo
Camp Echo, Diwaniyah, Iraq, Wednesday October 5, 2005

The next morning as I was walking to the shower building past last night's fire ring I noticed three 82mm mortar shells that had been pulled from the ashes of the fire. I wondered first of all why I didn't see them last night, and secondly, why they were there at all. But maybe it was best that I didn't know the answer to either of those questions.

After training the ROC computer operator all morning, I packed my gear and hopped into the 4-door armored blue Toyota pickup for the short ride back to the helipad with Glen from the ROC. Two Blackhawks were already on the ground refueling when we got there. I noticed a familiar looking unit arm patch on one of the crew members so I asked where he was from. He said, "I'm from Connecticut, but our aviation battalion is part of the Montana National Guard." I said, "Anyone here from Montana?" He said, "Yeah, your pilot over there is from Montana." So I went over to the pilot and asked him his name and where he was from. CPT Scott Bare was from Kalispell and just returned from leave two weeks ago. "Funny," I said, "same here." As it turns out Scott lives in Creston but of course he knew Glen Conklin (a distant relative of mine) in Kalispell and my Montana Army National Guard helo pilot neighbor Don Sneck who was over here last year.

So CPT Scott fixed me up with some headphones, put me in a window seat and asked if I had ever been to Babylon. I replied I had never flown over this area before. So he said, "After we stop at the U.S. Consulate in Hilla we will fly over Babylon so you can get a look at it." It was a good trip and I promised I would drop by and see him and the other Montana Guard folks at their battalion headquarters in Balad the next time I got up that way. But tonight I'm scheduled to fly on the "Grey Goose" to Fallujah with the Marines.

Dave Conklin and CPT. Scott Bare, 1-189th Aviation Battalion Pilot with the Montana National Guard meet at Camp Echo, Multinational Division-Central South Headquarters, Diwaniyah, Iraq. Wednesday Oct 5, 2005. (DSCN1615) (Photo --Dave Conklin)

Return to Ramadi

Camp Blue Diamond, 2nd Marine Division Headquarters, Ramadi, Iraq, Saturday October 8, 2005

The Wild West of Iraq is Marine country. Just like my first trip here in the spring, Marine country is easy to get to but hard to leave. I rode space-A in the CH-46 "Grey Goose" Marine helicopter to Fallujah where I loaded a computer and trained three operators on the new software. My next hop would be to Camp Blue Diamond in Ramadi. It is a small camp and a well-known "hotspot" in the middle of bad guy land. Yet getting to this place that no one wants to go to is always difficult. The 2nd Marine Expeditionary Force, or "second MEF" as the Marines here call their headquarters, was in the middle of rotating back to Camp Lejeune, North Carolina and helicopter seats are at a premium.

After I finished maintaining and loading their computer I went over to the LMCC to see my friend GySgt Dale Swink who was also about to rotate back to Camp Lejeune himself. Then I stopped at MHG to check on flights to Al Taqqadum, or "TQ" as the Marines call it, where I was hoping to link up with Chris Branum. He is our Tapestry guy with the Marines there and a former Marine himself.

I had a choice of three flights out of Fallujah but an unexploded mortar closed the Landing Zone. The next night, as a space-A traveler, I was again left behind. Luckily last night I was able to get on an unscheduled CH-46 helicopter flight that landed at Camp Blue Diamond in Ramadi at 11:30 p.m. I signed in at the plywood shack that serves as the passenger terminal and stumbled down the dark street to look for the Aegis building near the motor pool. I was happy they left the back door open and I was soon occupying an empty bunk bed.

Today was another train and maintain day, and at Blue Diamond the sound of the birds in the reeds of the Euphrates River and in the Eucalyptus trees and Date Palms is often punctuated by incoming or outgoing artillery fire. Everyone here wears body armor and a helmet (known as IBA and Kevlar) anytime they are outside. On our way to lunch I asked a food service worker what the flagpole with the red flag at the top was for. He said that meant watch for incoming. Not long after, I jumped as I heard the first of 5 artillery rounds go off. So did the birds as a huge flock lifted off of the bombed out palace down the street. Luckily these rounds were outgoing. The rule of thumb is if you feel them in your feet, they are outgoing, but if you feel them in your chest they are incoming.

At dusk the Aegis team finally returned from Camp Victory with their repaired GMC. By 9:00 p.m. I was packed up and walked back to LZ Spearhead to catch the first available CH-46 going to TQ that night.

The sun sets over the Euphrates River near the west gate of Camp Blue Diamond, 2nd Marine Division Headquarters, Ramadi, Iraq. According to the Islamic tradition of Ramadan, which began with the new moon (on Oct 5th this year), food cannot be consumed until after the sun sets. Saturday Oct 8, 2005. (DSCN1630) (Photo -- Dave Conklin)

The Second Battle of Trafalgar
Liberty Pool, Green Zone, Baghdad, Saturday October 22, 2005

My friend and ex-British naval officer "Captain Jack" who works here at the PCO told me he had been in a "pissing match" for a long time with his boss. So Jack decided to hand in his letter of resignation and booked himself a flight around the world—starting now and ending next spring sometime. For the price of about $2,500 he bought a ticket that included layovers in Paris, Bangkok, Los Angeles, and New York with plenty of time to spend his savings.

So on the last weekend of his employment he decided to host a going away party at the swimming pool in the Green Zone. But this was no ordinary party. It was to include barbequed chicken, beer, a tub of rum to "splice the main brace" and, right here in Liberty Pool, a celebration of the 200th anniversary of the famous Battle of Trafalgar.

For those who are not up to date on British naval history, Trafalgar is one of the most famous naval battles in the history of warfare. On October 21, 1805, off of Cape Trafalgar near Cadiz, Spain, Admiral Lord Nelson of the Royal Navy, with 26 frigates and men-of-war attacked the combined French and Spanish fleet of 40 ships, killing over 4,000 men and sinking or disabling most of their ships. This battle secured the supremacy of the British navy on the high seas for the next hundred years.

For a week now, Jack had been secretly building ships for each navy in his room. Every time he went to eat at the dining hall he would steal a few plastic spoons for masts and styrofoam to-go plates for ship hulls. Then he took stones from the road for ballast and duct taped them to the spoons. Finally he printed the appropriate flags, and taped them to the top of the spoons as sails and flags.

Tonight we brought the combined navies to the pool. Just as in the first battle of Trafalgar, the drums rolled, we all took a last swig of rum, and prepared the fleets for battle. The first to go into the pool were the two columns of the French and Spanish fleet, all 40 ships, tied nicely together with twine. Next came the 29 ships of the British fleet, battleships of styrofoam to-go plates, and frigates of more aerodynamically shaped oval plastic cake plates.

Again as historically accurate as possible, we climbed into the treacherous waters of the wading pool to position the two French and Spanish columns to the leeward and the British fleet to the windward on a heading to split the enemy in half and scatter their ships. But unlike the first battle, just as this one was to begin the wind died and the fleets were becalmed.

Jack was beside himself but soon found a long garden hose to create the flow needed to literally wash the British fleet on a collision course with the French. Since real gunpowder was not allowed at Liberty Pool, Jack now turned his garden hose into a water cannon to finish off the French and Spanish fleet one ship at a time. This of course was followed by the old English tradition of a rainstorm for all the spectators—created again by Jack's garden hose. So this my friends is how we in Iraq celebrated the 200th anniversary of the Battle of Trafalgar and the loss of a fine fellow-in-arms to hopefully safer and saner places.

John "Captain Jack" Salutes under the Royal Navy Ensign flag on his last night shift in Baghdad, Iraq. Wednesday Oct 12, 2005. (DSCN1656) (Photo -- Dave Conklin)

17. The Fight Goes On

*Let your interest be in the opportunity that you snatch
and not in the opportunity that was given to you.*
– Translated Inscription above Presidential Palace Door

Class Today, *Insha'Allah*
Projects and Contracting Office, Green Zone, Sunday November 13, 2005

My workday began at 6:30 a.m. as usual. After a short walk to my LMCC office trailer from my room I checked to be sure the internet was up, vehicle position reports were coming in, and called our 24-hour Help Desk in San Diego on Skype to see if there were any issues on their end. At 7:30 a.m. I went over to the ROC to check their systems, followed by a trip to the dining hall for some corn flakes with boxed milk and orange juice.

At our daily 10-minute update I announced that I am again signing up for the class that the Comtech guys were teaching on how to operate their MTS transponders they sell to the PSD teams. This was important because we integrate their position reports into our mapping software that shows where all of the civilian vehicles are. People are always getting our two companies mixed up and I field lots of questions on how transponders work and how we "see" them with our software. They also let me have an MTS satellite-linked control station next to my desk for testing and as a backup for when the internet goes down.

I had been promising the Comtech guys (Kent, Lewis, Brad, and Mike) for months that I would take their 4-hour class as soon as they had an opening when there were no emergencies going on and if "I had time" or as the Iraqis say, "*Insha' Allah*" (God willing). The class began at 1 p.m. and I was one of three who could come today. Brad had just finished his PowerPoint slide show introduction when we heard the first BOOM. Since it wasn't REAL loud, we continued. Then about a minute later came the next, and louder, BOOM which was followed by an even louder CRACK!

We stayed put for a while, since inside is always better than outside in a mortar attack. Then, as the loud speakers known as "The Big Voice" finally blurted out "Take Cover" we knew the attack was over and I went outside to take a look. I could see a cloud of dust near the east wall of the compound about 25 feet away and the guard in the guard tower nearby pointed excitedly to the ground but I couldn't see any damage, only a small hole next to the wall.

I am standing 25 feet from my office with my hand on the tree that was split by a rocket coming from the south over the PCO compound fence at 1:30 p.m., about an hour ago. The rocket scorched the wall and made the hole on the lower left burying itself without exploding. Sunday Nov 13, 2005. (DSCN1831) (Photo --Dave Conklin)

From the low angle it appeared to be a rocket fired from the south, about a mile away on the other side of the Tigris River. It just missed the top of the south fence, split the crotch in a small tree, scorched the wall below, and buried itself so deep in the ground that the EOD guys who arrived later that day to check it out quit looking for it and just left it there. The loud crack was the rocket hitting the ground without exploding. We were locked down for the next two hours, thus again getting me out of the class I had been promising to take for so many months and again confirming my reputation as one of the most dangerous men in Baghdad.

Here is the official Report the ROC (Reconstruction Operations Center) sent out:

Subject: UXO Landed in the PCO Compound, EOD tasked

Just wanted to update everybody on what happened over the last hour or so. We had a total of 3 rounds hit in our immediate vicinity. One landed and exploded in the CASH [Combat Support Hospital] Annex. Three minor injuries to LNs (Local Nationals) and minor damage to a building (shed). The second round impacted in the neighborhood of the CASH (we believe behind it). This round did not initially explode but did detonate a little while later. There were no reported injuries from this round. The third round landed within our compound on the west side of the street. This round did not explode. EOD responded and determined that the round was too deep to dig out and that since it went through a couple of tree limbs and then buried itself without going off, that there was a low likelihood of it going off and, even if it did, it is deep enough that it probably will do no harm. It was deemed safer to leave it in place rather than try to dig it out.

Per the GRD/PCO G3, nobody is authorized to go down to the location of the unexploded round and check it out. There is nothing to see anyway other than a divot in the ground covered with sand. In addition to those rounds described above, an estimated 4 rounds impacted in the vicinity of the Palace. We have no information as of yet on casualties or damage but will keep you posted with anything we receive that is not classified.

And here is the "unofficial" report e-mailed to my colleagues by one of the guys at the Yorktown Tapestry Solutions, Inc. office who had recently visited me here:

My advice on protecting yourself against indirect fire is: stay clear of Dave Conklin – judging by my last visit, he attracts mortars and rockets. He had one mortar go off near his accommodations and I am convinced that the other attacks happened along his nocturnal jogging route. Maybe raise the issue with Jack and get him to give Dave his own isolated office somewhere in the IZ. Also, be careful of any invites to back street restaurants – at least go with a hard hat and armor.

Nb: - There may be more to this than first meets the eye and I feel there is a political motive. Dave is, after all, the self-styled "Mayor" of the IZ. Judging by all the people he knows around town, I would tread carefully.

A Traditional Thanksgiving
Falcon Group Compound, Baghdad, Iraq, Thursday November 24, 2005

Thursday dawned bright and sunny. The sun was just coming up over the Ishtar Sheraton Hotel in downtown Baghdad as I walked to the dining hall from my office at 7:30 a.m. Fall was in the air but you couldn't tell by looking at the leaves turning yellow, as palm leaves don't turn yellow, so you could only tell by the chill in the air. It was the coldest morning yet at about 45 F. As I walked, two CH-46 helicopters lifted off from the Hospital helipad and flew over my head with their rear cargo doors open as usual. I felt sorry for any Marines on board because I remember my rides on these helos last winter as being some of the coldest trips I endured.

The chilly weather and occasional small arms fire in the distance reminded me of my traditional Thanksgiving back home in Montana, which is also the last week of hunting season. The difference being that we shoot only turkeys and deer and don't have our rifles on fully automatic. For me there was no sleeping-in today. Supply convoys were on the road that had to be tracked by our software. The situation was complicated by the announcement that the electrical panel, and therefore internet, would be shut down in the main building for generator maintenance.

The day started well enough, but at 10:19 a.m. a PSC convoy escort team passing by Fallujah on the way to the Marine base at Al Assad had a flat tire and while they were fixing it they were engaged by small arms fire and RPGs. They thought they had it under control so didn't activate their panic alarm, but then once under way again they hit an IED and were attacked again at which time they did push the alarm. It was good they did because they had no radio or cell phone communication and were in a firefight for the next 20 minutes. We called the Marines who sent a QRF and evacuated one guy with a concussion from the IED. In the meantime they killed at least three insurgents including one on a rooftop with an RPG. The PSC's Ops manager Cynthia came by today and said that her convoy made it to Al Assad, dropped off their cargo, and finally made it back to Baghdad, at which time one of the remaining escorts handed in his resignation.

By the way, I was the Tapestry rep for the Thanksgiving party hosted by Falcon Group at their villa last night north of the Al Rasheed Hotel. Several PSC reps attended including Cynthia and her assistant Mark. I don't exactly know how the conversation got around to it but it turns out that Mark is under indictment for shipping a footlocker full of hand grenades back to the states. He said the CID folks were waiting for him when he went to pick up mail at the post office here. Apparently he was tasked to ship home some footlockers for guys who were fired. So he just put labels on them and took them all to the post office—without looking inside. One of the footlockers was not personal equipment but instead the one they kept full of ammunition and thermite grenades. So FBI agents were knocking on doors back in the states and Mark had some explaining to do.

By 1 p.m. operations were slowing down and we were able to join the troops from the hospital and engineers in the dining hall for Thanksgiving dinner complete with "pressed" turkey, dressing, sweet potato pie and a Dixie cup full of eggnog. A British colleague Tim joined us in the long line of folks waiting for the traditional meal. We were very impressed by all the Thanksgiving decorations which included miniature tepees and two date palms made by stacking pineapples for the trunk, adding small palm leaves, and hanging grapes for dates. Tim remarked that he was very impressed by the quality and amount of food that KBR (Kellogg, Brown & Root) was able to deliver on a regular and sustained basis. We all agreed that despite their getting a bad reputation from time to time, KBR was one of the few companies that could do a quality job on everything from building camps to feeding people on a long-term basis in a war zone.

After dinner everyone wanted to get outside so we borrowed a pickup truck and went over to FOB Blackhawk, near the PX, to pick up a computer to load our software for the PSC that does the tracking for MNSTC-I (Multinational Security Transition Corps-Iraq). FOB Blackhawk, at the bombed out Believers Palace, was totally different from the military camp I saw there last year. The old Russian BMPs are gone and it has been split into two camps for private contracting firms. The main villa with its marble floors and gilded toilets had been renovated for VIP lodging. It was an oasis in the middle of the chaos of the Green Zone.

After we retrieved the computer, I took Mike and Dan to Checkpoint 12 where the car bomb went off last month. We then drove to FOB

Prosperity where three huge metal Saddam busts that were removed from the palace still stand in the tank park. We took some photos of them and then drove back, stopping at the tomb of the Unknown Soldier for some sunset photos. We finished up the day with a dinner of pressed turkey leftovers at the dining hall and went back to the office for a while before turning in early.

Dave inspects a burned out car left from the October VBIED attack at CP-12 (Checkpoint 12) on the west end of Baghdad's Green Zone. Thursday Nov 25, 2005. (DSCN1859) (Photo --Dave Conklin)

Last Days in Baghdad
Projects and Contracting Office, Green Zone, Sunday January 8, 2006

Today I write my last postcard home to Montana after packing for a C-130 flight to Kuwait to catch a commercial airliner. After nearly two years in Iraq, I am finally going home. I know there is more to be done and that I will not be here to see it. But I hope that my work will contribute in some way to heal the wounds of war and help the Iraqis rebuild their country. I am proud to have met with, worked with, and made friends with some of the bravest men and women in the U.S. military, in Iraq, and in many other countries. I was fortunate to be a part of their lives for a while as we formed bonds based on our common experiences that transcended race, religion, and nationality. I share with them the hope that the war will end soon, *"Insha' Allah"* (God willing).

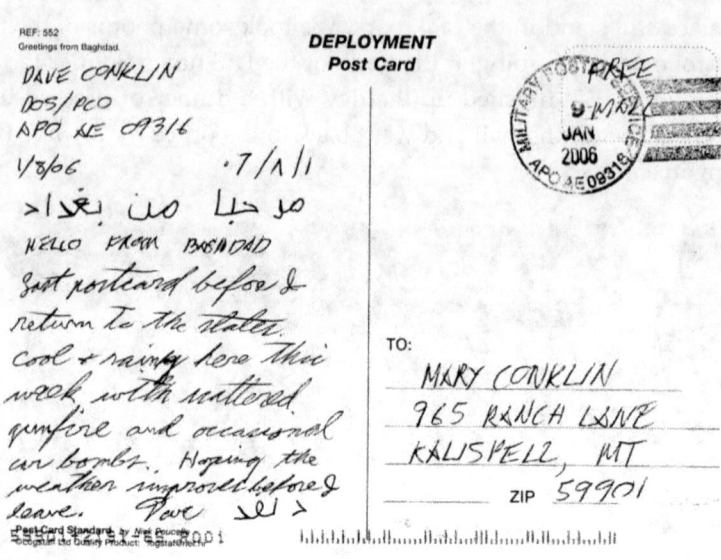

I send my last postcard home before leaving Baghdad Sunday, January 8, 2006. (Photo --Dave Conklin)

Acknowledgements

First of all, I would like to thank my family and friends who encouraged me to write about my daily activities and observations during my deployments to Iraq, no matter how trivial they seemed to me at the time. I also want to thank them for responding to my letters and providing their support, as well as their thoughts and viewpoints, which I have tried to incorporate into this journal.

This memoir would not have been possible without the brave and selfless men and women of the 350th Civil Affairs Command, as well as the countless reservists, National Guard members, and civilians who volunteer for duty to support our troops whenever and wherever they are deployed.

Also thanks to my friends and colleagues at Tapestry Solutions headquarters, and their other Field Support Engineers in Iraq and Kuwait for their support, assistance, local knowledge, and gracious hospitality whenever and wherever I needed it. Even if it meant sharing their quarters with me in a bombed-out concrete bunker at Al Taqqadum Air Base.

My sincere thanks also to the men and women of the private security companies who provided the first line of defense for daily logistics convoys through hostile areas in Iraq, and who provided my personal protection while traveling to their outposts so that I could provide them with the technology necessary to track their assets.

Also many thanks to all of my proofreaders including Beth Smith, Jody Johnson, and COL Mel Howry (Ret.) for their valuable comments and corrections. All illustrations not credited were provided by the author or from public domain sources.

Thanks to all of you who have provided me with your feedback on this memoir, and your encouragement and interest in learning more about my experiences during my deployment to Iraq during the Operation Iraqi Freedom years of 2004 and 2005. Any errors or omissions, however, are mine alone.

November 2023

Glossary

Military Acronyms & Abbreviations:

2IC	Second in command
AIF	Anti-Iraqi forces
AK-47	Military assault rifle (Russian)
Apache	AH-64 attack helicopter
BDU	Battle dress uniform
BIAP	Baghdad International Airport
Blackhawk	UH-60 utility helicopter
C-17	Globemaster 4-jet engine military cargo aircraft
C-130	4-propeller engine military cargo aircraft
C9	CMO (Civil-military operations)
Chinook	CH-47 U.S. Army tandem rotor cargo helicopter
CJTF	Combined joint task force
Grey Goose	CH-46 U.S. Marines tandem rotor cargo helicopter
CPA	Coalition Provisional Authority
CSH	Combat support hospital
DCU	Desert camouflage uniform
ECP	Entry control point
EOD	Explosive ordnance detachment
FOB	Forward Operating Base
FSE	Field support engineer
GDMS	Global distribution management system
Humvee	(HMMWV) High-mobility multipurpose wheeled vehicle
IBA	Interceptor body armor
IED	Improvised explosive device
IZ	International zone (Green Zone)
KBR	Kellogg, Brown & Root company
LMCC	Logistics Movement Coordination Center
LN	Local national (person)
LZ	Landing zone
MEDEVAC	Medical evacuation
MNF-I	Multi-national forces-Iraq

M4	Military assault rifle (carbine)
M16	Military assault rifle
MOS	Military occupational specialty
MP	Military Police
MRE	Meal ready to eat (field rations)
OIF	Operation Iraqi Freedom
PCO	Projects and Contracting Office
PSC	Private security company
PSD	Private security detail
QRF	Quick reaction force
ROC	Reconstruction operations center
RPG	Rocket-propelled grenade
SUV	Sport utility vehicle
TTAD	Temporary tour of active duty
VBIED	Vehicle-borne improvised explosive device

Military Ranks (common abbreviations in rank order):

NCO	Non-commissioned officer
PFC	Private first class
SGT	Sergeant
SSG	Staff sergeant
SFC	Sergeant first class
MSG	Master sergeant
SGM	Sergeant major
CSM	Command Sergeant Major
1LT	First lieutenant
CPT	Captain
MAJ	Major
LTC	Lieutenant colonel
LCDR	Lieutenant commander
COL	Colonel
CDR	Commander
BG	Brigadier general
MG	Major general
LTG	Lieutenant general

References

Associated Press. (2004, June 5). Iraq's New Prime Minister Calls for Halt to Attacks on Americans. *AP News, Baghdad*.

Carroll, A. (Ed.). (2006). *Operation Homecoming*. New York, NY: Random House.

Guerra, A. (2021). *Mexico's De la Huerta Rebellion: A Veteran's Chronicle*. (D. G. Conklin, Ed., & D. G. Conklin, Trans.) Kalispell, MT: Published privately by the editor; Moore Graphics, Youngtown, Arizona.

Jorgensen, C. (2012). *Great Battles: Decisive Conflicts That Have Shaped History*. New York, NY: Parragon Ltd.

Poitras, L. (Producer), Poitras, L. (Writer), & Poitras, L. (Director). (2004). *Flag Wars* [Motion Picture]. NY.

Poitras, L. (Producer), Poitras, L. (Writer), & Poitras, L. (Director). (2006). *My Country, My Country* [Motion Picture]. NY.

Washington Post. (2004, May 6). The Abu Graib Story. *Washington Post*. Retrieved May 4, 2004, from www.washingtonpost.com.

Zoroya, G. (2004, Apr 30). Iraq's Deadliest Month. *USA Today*, p. 1.

Index

1

11th Marine Expeditionary Force, 121
136th Finance Company, 84
1960 DeSoto, 97
1st Armored Division, 32, 45, 64, 65, 135
1st Cavalry Division, 77, 94, 119, 121

2

2nd Armored Cavalry Regiment, 53
2nd Marine Expeditionary Force, 181, 196

3

31st Combat Support Hospital. *See* Ibn Sina Hospital
350th CACOM. *See* 350th Civil Affairs Command
350th Civil Affairs Command, iii, iv, i, 6, 9, 25, 27, 28, 36, 57, 85, 86, 108, 113, 118, 122, 124, 125, 126, 127, 137, 146, 152, 153, 161, 207, 215
353rd Civil Affairs Command, 139, 152
372nd Mobile Public Affairs, 32

4

415th Civil Affairs Battalion, 38, 113
422nd Civil Affairs Battalion, 31
425th Civil Affairs Battalion, 26

5

57th Signal Battalion, 94

A

Abu Ghraib Prison, 78, 89
Acqavella, Kristen, 61, 74, 118, 124, 125, 131
Actis, John "Doc", 19
Aegis Defence Services, 166, 173, 192
Al Jaburi, Melad, 62, 123, 152
Al Neamy family, 34, 35, 36
Al Quadisiya District, 92
Al Rasheed Hotel, 32, 33, 48, 49, 50, 53, 60, 63, 64, 73, 111, 141, 145, 188, 204
Al Sadr, Moqtada, 63, 64, 120, 122
Al Taqqadum, 196, 207
Al Zarqawi, 33, 96, 100, 101, 143, 145
Ali al-Salem Air Base, 154, 155
Allawi, Iyad, 105
Al-Ziewa Neighborhood Clinic, 136
Ambush, 63, 65, 70, 74, 76, 88, 95, 100, 147, 168, 186
Ashoura festival, 45, 121
Assassin's Gate, 53, 57, 58

B

Babin, Todd, 94, 95, 118, 119, 125, 146, 152
Baghdad International Airport, 6, 7, 29, 87, 91, 92, 114, 118, 145, 153, 179, 180, 183, 208
Bariq Trading Company, 124, 129, 130, 161
Barn Owl, 112
Basrah, 88, 167, 179, 183, 192, 193
Believers Palace, 204
Beller, Tina, 1, 146
Blackwater PSC, 173
Bourdon, James, 112, 113, 114

Bremer, Paul, 105
Bronze Star, 6, 148, 215

C

Camel spider, 78
Camp Arifjan, 22, 158, 163
Camp Blue Diamond, 196, 197
Camp Doha, 113, 117, 118, 154, 155, 156, 157, 158, 159
Camp Echo, 193, 194, 195, 196
Camp Udairi, 22, 23, 24, 25, 26, 27, 53
Camp Victory, 38, 55, 58, 67, 80, 92, 94, 99, 100, 101, 131, 145, 153, 171, 172, 183, 184, 189, 197
Camp Wolf Pack, 52, 53, 58
Christy, Mark, 171, 180, 181, 183, 193
Comtech, 189, 200
Conklin, Dave, iv, 10, 11, 12, 14, 16, 17, 21, 22, 24, 25, 27, 28, 29, 30, 32, 35, 37, 38, 41, 50, 53, 56, 58, 61, 62, 66, 67, 69, 74, 76, 77, 80, 85, 86, 89, 93, 100, 108, 111, 116, 118, 119, 125, 127, 130, 137, 140, 142, 144, 146, 147, 153, 155, 156, 158, 159, 160, 161, 164, 165, 167, 168, 170, 172, 176, 178, 180, 183, 184, 187, 188, 191, 192, 194, 196, 197, 201, 202, 205, 206, 215
Conklin, David Gene. *See* Conklin, Dave
Culbreth, Shane, 179, 180
Cunningham, David, 152, 154

D

Dangerous Dave, 105
Davidson, BG Charles, 104, 105, 125
Dishdasha, 149, 150
Doc. *See* Actis, John
Domenech, John, 9, 108
Drozdowski, Gary, 84

Dunne, Mike, 124, 139, 144, 153, 154
Durnell, Craig, 50, 58, 63, 67

F

Fallujah, 31, 63, 64, 65, 67, 68, 70, 81, 82, 110, 125, 181, 183, 184, 185, 195, 196, 203
flu, 11, 84, 107, 108, 110
FOB Dragoon, 65
FOB Highlander, 94
FOB Prosperity, 205
Fort Bragg, 9, 10, 11, 12, 13, 14, 16, 19, 21, 22, 140, 150, 155, 160, 161

G

Green Zone, 6, 7, 8, 29, 30, 31, 32, 36, 41, 42, 43, 48, 49, 52, 53, 56, 57, 58, 59, 60, 64, 66, 69, 73, 74, 75, 77, 78, 80, 84, 85, 87, 89, 91, 94, 99, 100, 101, 102, 103, 104, 105, 107, 110, 111, 118, 119, 120, 122, 125, 127, 129, 136, 139, 142, 143, 144, 146, 147, 150, 152, 155, 163, 164, 165, 166, 169, 172, 183, 184, 185, 187, 188, 189, 190, 191, 193, 194, 198, 200, 204, 205, 208
Grenade attack, 45, 65, 84, 209
Grey Goose, 195, 196, 208

H

Hash House Harriers, 42, 149, 151
Higgenbotham, Chad "Higgie", 19
Higgie. *See* Higgenbotham, Chad
Hookah pipe, 59
House Armed Services Committee, 123, 125, 127
Howry, Mel, 122, 158
Hussein, Saddam, 4, 28, 30, 35, 69, 97, 117, 133
Hussein, Uday, 15, 32, 143, 144

I

Ibn Sina Hospital, 36, 84, 93, 163, 164, 184
IED, 33, 58, 64, 74, 87, 88, 92, 100, 103, 155, 192, 203, 208
International Zone. *See* Green Zone
Iraqi Airways, 132, 133
Ishtar Sheraton Hotel, 203

J

Joint Contracting Office, 8, 31, 36, 46, 114, 130

K

Karada District, 55, 133, 136
Karada Youth Center, 133, 137
Katyusha rockets, 49
Kellogg, Brown & Root Company, 53, 204, 208
Khor Az Zubaiya, 177, 179
King Faisal II., 111
Kochovski, Sergei, 165
Korean Embassy, 145, 146, 147
Kozy Bear. *See* Khor Az Zubaiya
Kuwait City, 22, 23, 25, 28, 113, 117, 118, 154, 157, 158, 177, 179

M

Maree, James, 153
Mississippi National Guard, 19
Montana National Guard, 159, 195
Montini, Frank, 175
Moser, Anthony, 180
Mosul, 39, 74, 82, 110, 113, 119, 167

N

Najaf, 65, 67, 120, 122, 193, 194

Nickel-plated AK-47, 143

O

Office trailer contract, 129, 130, 200

P

Parker, Alan, 172, 173
Perkins, Will, 19, 147
Poitras, Laura, 104
Presidential Palace, 29, 37, 43, 52, 74, 84, 85, 94, 96, 98, 99, 103, 105, 123, 140, 146, 150, 163, 164, 171, 175, 181, 192, 200
Public Warehouse Company, 177, 178, 179
Pylypuw, Rich, 108

R

R&R leave, 104, 107, 116
Rasafa Health Center, 134
Razzook, Moyaad, 55, 59, 61, 73, 94, 99
Rodgers, George, 14, 19, 24
Route Irish, 31, 32, 38, 55, 56, 99, 100, 172, 173, 189

S

Sandstorm, 37
Shannon, Ireland, 159, 160
Shumate, Jared, 117, 118, 134
Siberian tiger, 15
Steel rain, 73
Sullivan, Sean, 31, 32, 60
Sutton, David, 46

T

Tahrir Square, 98

Tallil Air Base, 113, 114
Tapestry Solutions, Inc., 6, 167, 171, 172, 175, 181, 196, 202, 204, 207, 215
Tilley, Robin, 168
Titan Company, 60, 120, 143
Trafalgar, 198, 199
Triple Canopy PSC, 142, 143, 192

U

Umm Qasr, 177, 178, 179

W

Washington National Guard, 64, 124

About the Author

Lieutenant Colonel David G. "Dave" Conklin (Retired) has authored numerous books and magazine articles and is the editor and translator of *Mexico's De la Huerta Rebellion: A Veteran's Chronicle* (Guerra, 2021). An Army reservist and Montana resident for more than forty years, he is a retired park ranger who lives in the Flathead Valley. Conklin has BS and MS degrees in Forestry and an MBA.

After twenty-eight years as a commissioned officer Dave Conklin re-enlisted as an Army Staff Sergeant, volunteering for mobilization to Iraq in 2004 with the 350th Civil Affairs Command. Prior to that he was Chief of the Broadcast Section of the 111th Press Camp from 1999 to 2003.

From 1997 to 1999 Conklin served as Deputy Chief of a Military Liaison Team (MLT) to the Bulgarian armed forces for the United States European Command. Previous assignments include: Plans, Operations & Military Support Officer, and Regimental Engineer for the 163d Armored Cavalry, Montana Army National Guard (ARNG). In 1989 Conklin served as a National Guard Exchange Officer to the Federal Republic of Germany.

He is a graduate of the Engineer Officer Basic and Advanced Courses, the U.S. Army Command & General Staff College, and the Defense Information School. His awards and decorations include the Bronze Star Medal, Defense Meritorious Service Medal, Iraq Campaign Medal, Global War on Terrorism Service and Expeditionary Medals, and the Combat Action Badge as well as numerous others.

In his last civilian occupation before retiring, Conklin was a field support engineer in Iraq and later the Western Pacific and Southeast Asia for Tapestry Solutions, Inc., a U.S. Department of Defense contractor and computer software manufacturer.

www.ingramcontent.com/pod-product-compliance
Lightning Source LLC
Chambersburg PA
CBHW071239080526
44587CB00013BA/1686